D0442773

How to Audit the
Process-Based QMS

Also available from ASQ Quality Press:

After the Quality Audit: Closing the Loop on the Audit Process,
Second Edition
J. P. Russell and Terry Regel

The Internal Auditing Pocket Guide
J. P. Russell

Quality Audits for Improved Performance, Third Edition
Dennis R. Arter

Process Auditing Techniques Guide
J. P. Russell

Internal Quality Auditing
Denis Pronovost

Quality Audit Handbook, Second Edition
ASQ Quality Audit Division

To request a complimentary catalog of ASQ Quality Press publications,
call 800-248-1946, or visit our Web site at http://qualitypress.asq.org .

How to Audit the Process-Based QMS

Dennis R. Arter, Charles A. Cianfrani,
and John E. (Jack) West

ASQ Quality Press
Milwaukee, Wisconsin

How to Audit the Process-Based QMS
Dennis R. Arter, Charles A. Cianfrani, and John E. (Jack) West

Library of Congress Cataloging-in-Publication Data

Arter, Dennis R., 1947–
  How to audit the process-based QMS / Dennis R. Arter, Charles A.
  Cianfrani, and John E. (Jack) West.
      p. cm.
  Includes bibliographical references and index.
  ISBN 0-87389-577-0 (hardcover, case bound : alk. paper)
    1. Auditing, Internal—Methodology. 2. Total quality
  management—Evaluation. 3. Organizational effectiveness—Evaluation.
  4. Management—Evaluation. 5. ISO 9001 Standard. I. Cianfrani,
  Charles A. II. West, Jack, 1944– III. Title.

  HF5668.25.A77 2003
  657'.458—dc21   2003002635

© 2003 by ASQ

All rights reserved. No part of this book may be reproduced in any form or by any means, electronic, mechanical, photocopying, recording, or otherwise, without the prior written permission of the publisher.

10 9 8 7 6 5 4 3 2

ISBN 0-87389-577-0

Publisher: William A. Tony
Acquisitions Editor: Annemieke Koudstaal
Project Editor: Paul O'Mara
Production Administrator: Gretchen Trautman
Special Marketing Representative: Robin Barry

ASQ Mission: The American Society for Quality advances individual, organizational,
and community excellence worldwide through learning, quality improvement, and knowledge exchange.

Attention Bookstores, Wholesalers, Schools, and Corporations: ASQ Quality Press books, videotapes, audiotapes, and software are available at quantity discounts with bulk purchases for business, educational, or instructional use. For information, please contact ASQ Quality Press at 800-248-1946, or write to ASQ Quality Press, P.O. Box 3005, Milwaukee, WI 53201-3005.

To place orders or to request a free copy of the ASQ Quality Press Publications Catalog, including ASQ membership information, call 800-248-1946. Visit our Web site at www.asq.org or http://qualitypress.asq.org .

Printed in the United States of America

∞ Printed on acid-free paper

American Society for Quality

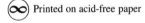

Quality Press
600 N. Plankinton Avenue
Milwaukee, Wisconsin 53203
Call toll free 800-248-1946
Fax 414-272-1734
www.asq.org
http://qualitypress.asq.org
http://standardsgroup.asq.org
E-mail: authors@asq.org

Copyright Protection Notice for the ANSI/ISO 9000 Series Standards:
These materials are subject to copyright claims of ISO, ANSI, and ASQ.
Not for resale. No part of this publiation may be reproduced in any form,
including an electronic retrieval system, without the prior written permission
of ASQ. All requests pertaining to the ANSI/ISO 9000 Series Standards
should be submitted to ASQ.

Note: As used in this document, the term "ISO 9001:2000" and all derivatives refer to the ANSI/ISO/ASQ Q9001-2000 series of documents. All quotations come from the American National Standard adoptions of these International Standards.

Table of Contents

List of Figures and Tables

Preface

This book is intended to help those involved in managing and conducting audits to ISO 9001:2000. It can be used as a guide to establishing a new audit program or for revitalizing one that has been operational for some time. It focuses on achieving an audit program that produces value-adding results for the organization.

To facilitate ease of use by the reader, this book consists of a general introduction followed by four parts:

Part I   Process-Based Internal Quality Auditing

Part II   Audit Program Management

Part III The Process of Auditing

Part IV   Aids to Audit Program Implementation

USING THIS BOOK

The user should first read the book in the order it is presented. As you read, refer to the items in part IV to understand how the concepts may look on paper. This gives a complete understanding of how the concepts can be adapted to a specific set of circumstances. Icons in the margins direct the reader to the appropriate items in Part IV. The items presented in Part IV include:

 Tools (forms or worksheets) that can aid in accomplishing a recommended activity

 Checklists that can be used to ensure that all activities have been considered.

 Questions that should be considered when auditing processes, functions, or specific requirements of ISO 9001:2000.

xix

We believe that the art and science of auditing quality management systems that have been designed and implemented following the process approach (the foundation of ISO 9001:2000) will be much more challenging and interesting than auditing 20 discrete elements to determine if documented procedures and records exist.

Auditing a process-based QMS, or even small elements of such a system, requires auditors to understand and integrate into an audit all aspects of organizational activities, from high-level planning through ensuring that customers are satisfied.

Indeed, the role of auditing is evolving, and the skills and competence required to do it well also need to evolve. We believe that the contents of this book will help auditors understand their role in the organization and to discharge their auditing duties in a way that is challenging to them and contributes to the success of the organization.

Part I

Process-Based Internal Quality Auditing

INTRODUCTION—THE BASICS OF PROCESS-BASED INTERNAL QUALITY AUDITING

Part I provides a broad overview of the basic elements of auditing, and specifically auditing ISO 9001:2000–based quality management systems. It discusses the concepts behind auditing, reviews audit principles, describes the process approach to quality management systems, addresses how to audit a process-based system, and reviews the two basic purposes for conducting audits.

This section is divided into four chapters. Chapter 1 addresses internal audit concepts, principles, and requirements. It defines auditing and provides a practical explanation of the principles that internal audit programs and auditors should use as their basic guides. It also covers the internal audit requirements of ISO 9001:2000 and discusses how those requirements should be applied.

Chapter 2 is dedicated to a detailed explanation of the process approach. It discusses the eight quality management principles that were used as key input for the development of ISO 9001:2000. It explains how organizations should use the process approach in developing their quality management systems. A complete understanding of these concepts is essential for auditors who will audit systems to the requirements of ISO 9001:2000.

Chapter 3 addresses auditing the process-based quality management system. It provides insight into the audit processes that can be used, and gives strategies for auditing a process-based system.

Chapter 4 provides an understanding of the distinction between auditing to ensure conformity to requirements and auditing for performance improvements.

1

Internal Audit Concepts, Principles, and Requirements

Periodic evaluations are essential to ensure the effective, ongoing implementation and improvement of any quality management system. Various types of evaluation techniques are used. Inspection, statistical process control (SPC), and product auditing are commonly used for products and processes. For quality management systems, the most common techniques are auditing, management review, and self-assessment.

Auditing is a process in which an objective and impartial evaluation is made of all or part of a quality management system's implementation against agreed-upon criteria. This chapter discusses the requirements for internal auditing as found in ISO 9001:2000, clause 8.2.2, *Internal audit*.

Internal quality audits are used to evaluate the adequacy of documents used to implement the quality management system, whether quality management system requirements are being met, and the effectiveness of system implementation. Audits can also be used to identify opportunities for improvement.

Internal audits are conducted by, or on behalf of, an organization for internal purposes and can form the basis for the organization's self-declaration of conformity. Supplier audits are conducted by customers of the organization or by other persons on behalf of a customer. Registration and government audits are conducted by external organizations outside of the typical customer–supplier relationship. All of these organizations can verify whether requirements, such as those of ISO 9001, are being met.

Management review of the quality management system is a process by which top management conducts regular, systematic evaluations of the suitability, adequacy, effectiveness, and efficiency of the quality management system with respect to the quality policy and objectives. This review is the subject of ISO 9001:2000, clause 5.6, *Management review*. The review process also should verify that the quality policy and quality objectives are aligned with and support achieving overall business policy and objectives. It can include consideration of the need to modify the quality policy and objectives in response to changing needs and expectations of interested parties. The management review includes determination of the need for actions to improve products and processes. Audit reports are among the sources of information used for this review of the quality management system.

Self-assessment is a process for comprehensive, systematic, and regular review of the organization's activities and results. We use the term to mean an evaluation in which the organization's activities and results are compared to performance improvement criteria such as ISO 9004:2000 or a model of excellence such as the criteria for the Malcolm Baldrige National Quality Award. Self-assessment methodology can provide an overall view of the performance of the organization, and the degree of maturity of the quality management system. It can also help to identify areas requiring improvement in the organization, and to determine priorities. Such self-assessments typically go beyond auditing against detailed requirements. In doing so, they look for opportunities for the organization to improve its efficiency and performance. Self-assessment is discussed in ISO 9004:2000, clause 8.2.1.5, *Self-assessment,* and a process for self-assessment is given in ISO 9004:2000, Annex A. Sometimes the term self-assessment is used differently to mean corporate internal audits (as practiced by operational or financial auditors) or assessment of personal values.

Some have argued the merits of one approach over the others. Organizations may wish to use all three since each has its own advantages. By its very name we can assume that self-assessment is normally performed by and for the organization being evaluated. This means that those who have the most extensive knowledge of the processes conduct the evaluation. The insight gained by these "insiders" can form the basis for fundamental process changes. Self-assessments tend to be very detailed examinations using high-level criteria most pertinent to the organization, and involve judgments on the maturity of the quality management system. They are generally conducted less frequently than the other two types of evaluations. Management review, on the other hand, involves an organization's top managers making determinations of their own system's sufficiency, adequacy, and effectiveness. Management reviews can use the results of self-assessments and audits as well as other data such as process performance trends and customer feedback. Audits are somewhat different in that they are, by definition, independent activities conducted against fixed requirements such as ISO 9001:2000 and methods used for local implementation. Management review and self-assessment are characterized by direct involvement of those responsible for the processes being examined. Audit, on the other hand, is characterized by the concept of independence. While the topic covered in this book is auditing, the authors believe that organizations should employ a mix of all three techniques.

AUDIT DEFINED

The concept of audit is defined by ISO 19011:2002 and by ISO 9000:2000 as:

"systematic, independent and documented process for obtaining audit evidence and evaluating it objectively to determine the extent to which audit criteria are fulfilled"

This is a very flexible and useful definition. This definition is general and does not mention quality. Let's elucidate the definition. Auditing is a process:

- For obtaining evidence (facts supported by credible data) related to the system, process, area, subject, or activity being audited

- For determining the extent to which the system, process, area, subject, or activity being audited meets some specified criteria

- That is conducted objectively and impartially

This definition provides a foundation for many of the concepts needed to manage and conduct audits.

AUDIT PRINCIPLES

Any quality management system internal audit program needs to be grounded in the principles that govern good auditing. There are a number of principles stated in ISO 19011:2002, *Guidelines for quality and/or environmental management systems auditing,* that can be used to guide the internal audit program and the internal auditors.

The principles deal with the overall integrity and operation of the audit program and the integrity of the program's auditors, as well as how audits are conducted.

a) Ethical conduct: the foundation of professionalism

Trust, integrity, confidentiality and discretion are essential to auditing.

b) Fair presentation: the obligation to report truthfully and accurately

Audit findings, audit conclusions and audit reports reflect truthfully and accurately the audit activities.

Significant obstacles encountered during the audit and unresolved diverging opinions between the audit team and the auditee are reported.

c) Due professional care: the application of diligence and judgment in auditing

Auditors exercise care in accordance with the importance of the task they perform and the confidence placed in them by audit clients and other interested parties. Having the necessary competence is an important factor.

Further principles relate to the audit, which is by definition independent and systematic.

d) Independence: the basis for the impartiality of the audit and objectivity of the audit conclusions

Auditors are independent of the activity being audited and are free from bias and conflict of interest. Auditors maintain an objective state of mind throughout the audit process to ensure that the audit findings and conclusions will be based only on the audit evidence.

e) Evidence-based approach: the rational method for reaching reliable and reproducible audit conclusions in a systematic audit process

Audit evidence is verifiable. It is based on samples of the information available, since an audit is conducted during a finite period of time and with finite resources. The appropriate use of sampling is closely related to the confidence that can be placed in the audit conclusions.

Figure 1.1   Principles from ISO 19011.

Source: BSR/ISO/ASQ QE 19011-2002. Used by permission.

The audit program should be able to achieve consistent results regardless of which auditor conducts a specific audit. Internal audits are a key input into top management's determination of the suitability and effectiveness of the quality management system. Management should be able to rely on the audit results to give a fair, accurate, and comprehensive picture of the quality management system. To ensure this consistency and reliability, the leaders of the audit program need to ensure that it evidences certain characteristics:

• *Objectivity.* The audit process should be set up so that personal feelings, opinions, or interests do not influence it. This means that the assignment of auditors must ensure that the individuals assigned to a particular audit can be objective. Naturally, this must be a key consideration in the determination of the individuals who are suitable for inclusion in the "pool" of available auditors.

• *Impartiality.* The audit program must not favor one part of the organization, one manager, or one process over others. The audit process should treat each part of the organization impartially. This includes audit scheduling, audit frequency, assignment of auditors, conduct of audits, and reporting of audit results.

• *Evidence-based focus.* The audit process should be focused on determining the truth. As with the legal system, auditing should attempt to determine "the truth, the whole truth, and nothing but the truth." But auditors are faced with limited time and resources, and truth can be elusive. To determine the absolute truth, it is necessary to consider all points of view. This just may not be possible given the constraints placed upon a particular audit. It means that auditors need to place most of their effort in determining the facts. The definition of the term "audit" includes the idea of obtaining evidence and comparing that evidence against criteria in an objective and impartial matter. It may be impractical or even impossible for the audit program to determine the "truth"—but it must at least get the facts straight. The audit evidence should be made up of facts supported by credible data. The audit evidence should be sufficient to justify any conclusions drawn from it. While audit evidence may be based on sampling, it is often not feasible to draw sufficiently large sample sizes to achieve high statistical confidence levels. This means that the auditor training process needs to ensure that auditors are capable of making good judgments as to sampling results.

• *Competency*. The audit program should ensure that auditors have the requisite skills, training, educational background, and experience to perform their assigned audits. Auditors should never be assigned to audit processes for which they are not qualified. The relationship between the audit boss and the auditors needs to be such that an auditor can fully discuss and obtain resolution of any audit situation in which he or she feels uncomfortable. The audit boss is that individual in the organization responsible for managing and leading the audit process.

• *Cooperation and trust*. While it is not mentioned in most lists of audit principles, the idea of trust is central to auditing for performance improvement. The audit boss must facilitate an environment of cooperation between auditors and auditees. This environment is such that auditors really do have performance improvement in mind as they gather their evidence. Without compromising the other audit principles, they focus on that which is good for the entire organization. Auditees need to feel that they too are part of the team and recognize audit results as key inputs to improving their own work management activities.

In addition to these principles for the audit program, auditors must abide by certain ethical principles in their work:

• *Professionalism*. Auditors must be diligent, conscientious, and skillful in their work.

• *Honesty*. Auditors must always be responsible and not withhold reporting of issues, nonconformities, or violations when sufficient evidence indicates they exist. Auditors must never support or participate in any activity that violates customer, statutory, regulatory, or internal requirements. They also need to be honest with the auditees.

• *Ethics*. Credibility of the audit process is maintained only if auditors adhere to ethical standards. Auditors must remember that their role is to discover evidence, compare it to criteria, and to reach reasonable conclusions regarding how well the criteria have been met. The role is not one of a consultant or advisor. Regardless of the objectives of an audit, auditors should focus on identification of issues and gaps and never provide advice as to how these issues should be addressed or what action should be taken to close the identified gaps.

• *Confidentiality*. Auditors need to be prudent in their use and protection of information they obtain during audits. Information gained in audits should never be used for personal gain in any way. Likewise, proprietary information that gives the organization a business advantage must be protected from unauthorized disclosure.

- *Duty to report.* Auditors may uncover evidence of fraud or other possible legal violations during their evaluations. They have a duty to report the matter to the audit boss, and to other officials inside or outside the organization (as appropriate) if action is not forthcoming. Of course, collected evidence should be protected for possible use in legal proceedings.

These audit principles are basic ideas or beliefs that must be observed in developing audit programs and in conducting audits. It is important for both auditors and those responsible for managing audit programs to keep these audit principles in mind. As we shall see, the internal audit requirements of ISO 9001:2000 reflect much of what is found in the principles stated above.

INTERNAL AUDIT REQUIREMENTS OF ISO 9001:2000

The internal audit requirements of ISO 9001:2000 are found in clause 8.2, *Monitoring and measurement,* so we can think of auditing as an activity that measures the implementation of the quality management system or of the system's parts.

Even as we recognize internal audit as a form of measurement, it continues to be an essential process to provide confidence in the effective implementation of the quality management system. Part II will discuss how to manage the overall audit program to meet the requirements of ISO 9001:2000, and to focus it on both ensuring that the quality management system meets requirements and continual improvement.

REQUIREMENTS FOR THE AUDIT PROGRAM

Auditing should be recognized as a valuable, ongoing process. A one-time set of audits to meet ISO 9001 requirements in order to obtain registration does not constitute an audit program. Internal quality audits should not be performed solely to prepare for visits by outsiders. Nor is it sufficient to conduct internal audits only when there are suspected problems. Audits must be scheduled and carried out on a periodic basis and at planned intervals. They should be used to determine whether the requirements of ISO 9001:2000 are being met and the degree to which the quality management system has been effectively implemented and maintained. Indicators of problems with the effectiveness of the quality management system may include the occurrence of high numbers of customer complaints or of high levels of scrap and rework within the organization. Clause 8.2.1 of ISO 9001:2000 requires organizations to monitor customers' perceptions as to whether customer requirements have been met. Internal auditors often use this information to identify product realization processes that require further investigation regarding the extent to which they have been effectively implemented and maintained. In a similar fashion, scrap and rework information may be of value for identifying subject areas for the internal audit.

Audits must be planned. This planning must take into account a number of factors including the importance and status of the processes and areas to be audited. The results of previous audits also need to be considered. The audit scope, frequency, and methodologies must be defined.

Whatever factors are considered, internal quality audits may be performed on parts of the quality management system or on the entire system. Audits may be performed by functional area (often called vertical audits) or by process (often called horizontal audits). The scope of each audit should be clear, and the audit methodology and frequency of audits within the audit program should be identified.

The auditing process must maintain independence. This means that it must ensure objectivity and impartiality. Certainly, auditors cannot be the individuals who perform the activity being audited. Internal auditors should be qualified to do their work. This is particularly necessary for "guest" auditors or technical experts who do not normally perform audits but are used to provide technical product or process expertise and may be inexperienced at auditing.

A written procedure is required to describe how audits are planned, conducted, and reported. The procedure must also address the records to be maintained. Audit results should be documented in a written report and records should indicate audit results including any deficiencies found.

All of the above audit program requirements are discussed in greater depth in Part II.

REQUIREMENTS FOR FOLLOW-UP
ON AUDIT RESULTS

ISO 9001:2000 requires that managers of the areas audited follow up on audit results. If problems are identified, corrective action must be taken in a timely manner. If audit results are good, follow-up should assure acceptable ongoing performance and continual improvement. The management system should establish normal time periods for responding to audit findings, such as 30 days. These normal periods might be reduced or extended for special circumstances. Audit results are required input to management reviews.

Follow-up actions should be evaluated to assure the effectiveness of corrective actions. This effectiveness should be reported to top management. The follow-up need not be part of the audit system if it is accomplished by other means. Auditors are generally involved in some way, however.

It may be useful for those who have used ISO 9001:1994 to compare the internal audit requirements of that standard with those of ISO 9001:2000. As can be seen in Table 1.1, we find only minor changes. Perhaps the most noteworthy changes may be the addition of scope, frequency, methods, criteria, and use of prior audit results in planning. While some organizations may see these as new requirements, many have included all of these in their audit programs for years. Some organizations may find the change in wording regarding the independence of auditors to be significant. But for the most part, there is no requirement in ISO 9001:2000 to change the way auditing is done.

Table 1.1 Comparison of ISO 9001-1994 and ISO 9001-2000 internal audit requirements.

ANSI/ISO/ASQC Q9001-1994 (4.17, Internal quality audits)	ANSI/ISO/ASQ Q9001-2000	Comments
The supplier shall establish and maintain documented procedures for planning and implementing internal quality audits to verify whether quality activities and related results comply with planned arrangements	The organization shall conduct internal audits at planned intervals to determine whether the quality management system a) conforms to the planned arrangements (see 7.1), to the requirements of this International Standard and to the quality management system requirements established by the organization, and	Very similar requirements for establishing procedures and conducting audits.
and to determine the effectiveness of the quality system.	b) is effectively implemented and maintained.	New requirement is for determination of implementation" rather than "determine the effectiveness of the quality system." ISO 9001:2000 leaves determination of effectiveness to top management as a part of management review.
	The responsibilities and requirements for planning and conducting audits, and for reporting results and maintaining records (see 4.2.4) shall be defined in a documented procedure.	Very similar to ISO 9001:1994.
Internal quality audits shall be scheduled on the basis of the status and importance of the activity to be audited and shall be carried out by personnel independent of those having direct responsibility for the activity being audited.	An audit programme shall be planned, taking into consideration the status and importance of the processes and areas to be audited, as well as the results of previous audits. The audit criteria, scope, frequency and methods shall be defined. Selection of auditors and conduct of audits shall ensure objectivity and impartiality of the audit process. Auditors shall not audit their own work.	New requirements include: • Inclusion of previous audit results in planning • Audit scopes • Audit frequency • Audit methods • Audit criteria Focus is on objectivity and impartiality of the audit process rather than just independence of auditors.

Continued

Continued

ANSI/ISO/ASQC Q9001-1994 (4.17, Internal quality audits)	ANSI/ISO/ASQ Q9001-2000	Comments
The results of the audits shall be recorded (see 4.16) and brought to the attention of the personnel having responsibility in the area audited. The management personnel responsible for the area shall take timely corrective action on deficiencies found during the audit.	The management responsible for the area being audited shall ensure that actions are taken without undue delay to eliminate detected nonconformities and their causes.	New requirement is more succinctly stated but essentially the same.
Follow-up audit activities shall verify and record the implementation and effectiveness of the corrective action taken (see 4.16).	Follow-up activities shall include the verification of the actions taken and the reporting of verification results (see 8.5.2).	Requirements are essentially the same when read with ISO 9001:2000 clause 8.5.2.
NOTES 20 The results of internal quality audits form an integral part of the input to management review activities (see 4.1.3).		ISO 9001:2000 now requires that audit results be used as an input to management review.
21 Guidance on quality-system audits is given in ANSI/ASQC Q10011-1-1994, ANSI/ASQC Q10011-2-1994, and ANSI/ASQC Q10011-3-1994.	NOTE See ISO 10011-1, ISO 10011-2 and ISO 10011-3 for guidance.	The ISO 10011 series will be replaced by ISO 19011.

Sources: ANSI/ISO/ASQC Q9001-1994 and ANSI/ISO/ASQ Q9001-2000. Used by permission.

2

The Process Approach

NEW FOCUS FOR QUALITY MANAGEMENT SYSTEMS

There have been significant changes in the focus of quality management systems over time. Many of these are reflected in ISO 9001:2000. They include:

- A change from an internal focus to a focus on the customer

- A change in emphasis from just "controlling" or "assuring" quality to quality management and improvement

- A change in attitude from quality as the sole purview of specialists to an attitude that everyone in the organization has something to contribute to quality

- A change from leadership of quality activities by staff people to leadership by top managers

- A change emphasizing the alignment of quality management with the quality policy of the organization

- A change from the idea that the quality management system is driven by documentation to a focus on managing its processes

- A shift from independence of quality control activities to their integration into production and service processes

Principle 1—Customer Focus

Organizations depend on their customers and therefore should understand current and future customer needs, should meet customer requirements, and should strive to exceed customer expectations.

Principle 2—Leadership

Leaders establish unity of purpose and direction of the organization. They should create and maintain the internal environment in which people can become fully involved in achieving the organization's objectives.

Principle 3—Involvement of People

People at all levels are the essence of an organization, and their full involvement enables their abilities to be used for the organization's benefit.

Principle 4—Process Approach

A desired result is achieved more efficiently when activities and related resources are managed as a process.

Principle 5—System Approach to Management

Identifying, understanding, and managing interrelated processes as a system contributes to the organization's effectiveness and efficiency in achieving its objectives.

Principle 6—Continual Improvement

Continual improvement of the organization's overall performance should be a permanent objective of the organization.

Principle 7—Factual Approach to Decision Making

Effective decisions are based on the analysis of data and information.

Principle 8—Mutually Beneficial Supplier Relationships

An organization and its suppliers are interdependent, and a mutually beneficial relationship enhances the ability of both to create value.

Figure 2.1   The eight quality management principles of ISO 9000:2000.
Source: ANSI/ISO/ASQ Q9000-2000. Used by permission.

Early in the process of writing ISO 9001:2000, it was recognized that much had changed in the way organizations go about achieving quality. A small working group was established to investigate these shifts and make recommendations as input to the development of what became the ISO 9000:2000 series. That group deliberated over a period of several years and collected information from around the world. The result was the eight quality management principles shown in Figure 2.1.

All eight principles are discussed further in chapter 5 of *The ASQ ISO 9000:2000 Handbook* and a brochure on them may be downloaded from the ISO Web site at: http://www.iso.ch . Remember, the principles provide ideas or concepts related to quality management systems, and were used to provide input to the revision process that resulted in ISO 9001:2000, but they are not a part of the quality management system requirements of that standard. While not a part of the standard, each of these principles is embodied to some extent in ISO 9001:2000. None are more obviously adopted as part of the requirements than the principles related to the "system approach to management" and the "process approach." The use of these two principles together is often generally referred to as the "process approach."

THE PROCESS APPROACH AS A CONCEPT

ISO 9001:2000 quality management systems are said to be "process based" which means that they are based on the process approach to management. This means that a good understanding of the process-based system concepts is important to effectively auditing the systems. Let's review the two underlying quality management principles related to the system and its processes in greater detail:

• *Process approach.* "A desired result is achieved more efficiently when activities and related resources are managed as a process." This principle is best understood when it is applied to an individual process. A process is nothing more than a collection of interrelated activities, see Figure 2.2. These activities are related because they act together to transform inputs into outputs. Effective and efficient operation of the transformation requires coordination between the activities and management of the mechanisms necessary to conduct them. Mechanism is just a technical word for resources. A process approach also requires application of control to ensure that requirements will be met.

Full understanding of the process approach requires an understanding of the linkage provided by a process between suppliers and customers.

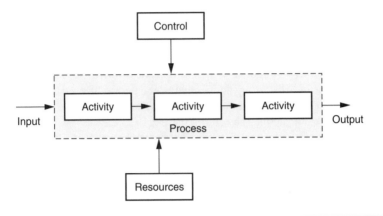

Figure 2.2   A process is a group of interrelated activities and related resources that transforms inputs to outputs.

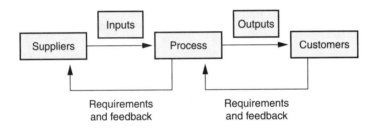

Figure 2.3   Suppliers provide inputs that the process transforms into outputs for customers.

Customers and suppliers can be either internal or external to the organization. Customers provide requirements to the process and feedback as to how well those requirements have been met. Likewise, the process provides requirements to its suppliers and feedback as to how well those requirements are met. This linkage is often referred to as SIPOC (suppliers, inputs, process, outputs, customers) and can be seen graphically in Figure 2.3.

   • *System approach to management.* "Identifying, understanding, and managing interrelated processes as a system contributes to the organization's effectiveness and efficiency in achieving its objectives." This principle applies to the whole quality management system. Thus, a system is a collection of interrelated processes with a common set of objectives and outputs. In essence, the quality management system is a group of interrelated processes focused on effectively and efficiently achieving the

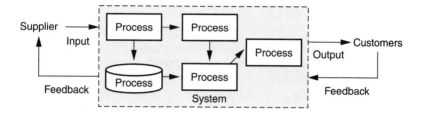

Figure 2.4   A system is a group of interrelated processes that work together to achieve outputs that meet objectives.

organization's quality objectives. Those objectives can be achieved without the system approach, but the principle indicates that they can be achieved more effectively and more efficiently if we manage the processes and their interactions together as a system. Figure 2.4 shows a basic system and its relationship to suppliers and customers.

These are the principles that provide a foundation for ISO 9001:2000. More-detailed requirements for implementation of the process approach to quality management as it is described in ISO 9001:2000 can be found in clauses:

- 4.1 Quality management system general requirements

- 5.4 Planning

- 7.1 Planning of product realization

- 7.5.1 Control of production and service provision

- 8.1 Measurement, analysis and improvements, general

When implementing quality management, organizations should consider the requirements contained in these clauses not only on an individual basis but also as a set of linked and interrelated requirements.

THE PROCESSES OF THE QUALITY MANAGEMENT SYSTEM

While we need to understand each of these clauses to fully appreciate the process approach, it is clause 4.1 that provides the basic requirements related to the concept. Clause 4.1 requires that the organization establish, document, implement, and maintain a quality management system. It also requires that the organization continually improve the effectiveness of that system. Clause 5.4 requires that the system be planned. Let's start our review of the detailed requirements with the planning process. Clause 5.4.1 requires that top management establish the organization's quality objectives, including those required to meet customer requirements for products and services. It also requires that these objectives be measurable and that they be deployed at the relevant functions and levels within the organization. These requirements for establishing and maintaining measurable quality objectives throughout the organization are fundamental to the proper implementation of a process-based quality management system. The objectives flow from the quality policy established by top management in accordance with clause 5.3. That policy determines the overall direction of the organization with regard to quality. The objectives support and facilitate achievement of the policy statements and make the policy much more than a collection of words with little relevance to the organization.

It is often said that measurement is the key to meeting top management's objectives related to quality. Or said another way: "what gets measured gets done." But meeting objectives also requires action. Having measurable objectives throughout the organization is not sufficient either for achieving top management goals or meeting the requirements of ISO 9001:2000. The quality management system is made up of processes. It is these processes that must be established, documented, implemented, maintained, and improved in such a way that the organization's quality objectives can be met. It is within these processes that action is taken to meet the objectives.

Clause 5.4.2 requires that top management plan the quality management system both to meet the requirements of ISO 9001:2000 and, more importantly, to meet the organization's own quality objectives. In planning the system, top management needs to ensure that the requirements of clause 4.1 are met.

It is in clause 4.1 that ISO 9001:2000 provides the basic requirements for implementing the process approach. The first requirement of clause 4.1 is to identify the processes needed for the quality management system and to understand how those processes are applied throughout the organization. Organizations have great flexibility in accomplishing this. They should focus on understanding the processes that are most important to achieving the quality objectives. In developing this understanding, it is common for organizations to start by preparing an overall process map or relationship map that pictorially depicts the top-level processes needed to manage for quality. Such a map can be used not only for understanding what processes make up the system, but also for illustrating how those processes work together so that their interactions can be understood and illustrated. It is not necessary that the processes of any organization's quality management

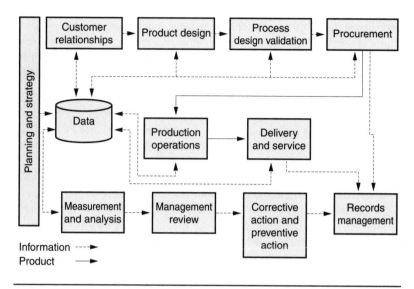

Figure 2.5   Example of a quality management system relationship map.

system reflect exactly the process structure given in ISO 9001:2000. In fact, it is probably best if the structure of the map, and therefore the system, fits the way the organization actually works. Figure 2.5 provides an example of such a map. The development of such a process map can be used as one of the key steps in the development of a quality manual.

Each of the system's processes must be managed. The process management requirements are outlined in clause 4.1 as follows:

• *Determining the criteria and methods needed to ensure effective operation and control the process.* We must understand the process outputs to understand what activities are necessary to control a process. Figure 2.3 illustrates this concept. One approach is to first identify the customers of the process and then work with those customers to understand the process outputs, how to measure those outputs, and reach agreement on targets for process performance. Next, identify the suppliers who provide inputs to the process. It's also useful to determine how these process inputs can be measured and establish targets for the inputs. This is often accomplished through dialogue with the suppliers. Once process inputs and outputs are clearly understood and their criteria established, the individual activities of the process can be described and a process flowchart can be prepared to show the individual activities. The process can also be described in a quality system procedure. The extent of this documentation should depend on consideration of items such as the complexity of the process, the competence level of its personnel, and the complexity of interactions among processes. There is a lot of flexibility regarding how processes can be documented and the extent to which the organization must go in providing documentation. The extent of required documentation is explained in the notes of clause 4.2 in ISO 9001:2000.

• *Monitoring and measurement of the process.* Processes require some form of monitoring and measurement. As with documentation, the extent to which the organization must go in monitoring and measurement of processes should depend on the nature of the process and its importance to the achievement of the organization's quality objectives. Certainly all processes should be monitored in some way; even if only by normal day-to-day supervision. On the other hand, those processes that are important to meeting customer requirements and the organization's quality objectives should be measured. There should be linkage between this measurement of the key processes and the overall quality objectives of the organization. For some processes, it may be appropriate to measure the output of individual activities or the actual parameters or characteristics of the process itself. Figure 2.6 illustrates where the process measurements may occur.

• *Analysis of the process.* Processes must be analyzed. This may be done by analyzing the data collected during process measurement activities. Sometimes, process analysis occurs on a day-to-day basis by process operators, by process engineers, or by personnel responsible for process supervision. This activity may use data generated during process operations or from any statistical process controls that may be used. The proper use of control charts in a manufacturing operation is one example of this sort of

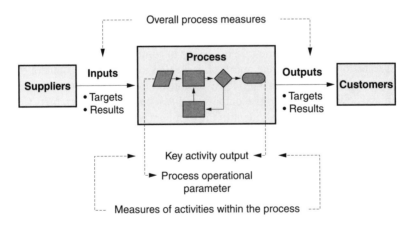

Figure 2.6 Measurement of processes.

on-the-job analysis. The preparation, analysis, and use of flowcharts to identify process disconnects and problems may also be helpful.

• *Ensuring that adequate resources are provided.* Adequate resources must be provided not only to operate the processes but also to carry out the control, monitoring, measurement, and improvement activities that have been planned. These resources include process equipment, people, information, work space, and anything else that may be necessary.

• *Implement the actions necessary to achieve results and improvement.* The key here is that all the planned activities must actually be carried out. It does no good to develop extensive process controls, plan for measurements to be used in improvement, and provide resources if these resources and plans are not actually used as intended.

PROCESS INTERACTIONS

Although it is important to understand the processes, it is equally important to understand and manage their interactions. This management of the processes together with their interactions is the key to use of the system approach to management. Some of these interactions are natural process "handoffs" to customers in the chain of processes needed for product realization. For example, there may be interactions between the product design process and the design validation process as well as the process for procurement of materials for production. There may be interaction between the procurement process and the process for production and delivery. This type of interaction is commonly understood, tends to be fairly obvious, and it is easy to describe or depict.

Other interactions commonly exist that may be less obvious. For example, the product design process may interact with the management review process, the corrective action process, the preventive action process, or the marketing process. Indeed, since preventive action is most effective when it is considered in early stages of product and process design, the interface between the product design and preventive action processes may be as critical to organizational success as the interface between product design and production. This type of interaction may occur infrequently, be difficult to describe, and may actually occur only if there is some initiating event such as a customer complaint. In the example chart given in Figure 2.5, this type of interaction is shown as a flow through the centralized data management process. Figure 2.7 is a more detailed chart showing one organization's product design process in greater detail, with additional interfaces. Notice that because of its criticality to the business, this organization has chosen to define design validation as a separate process.

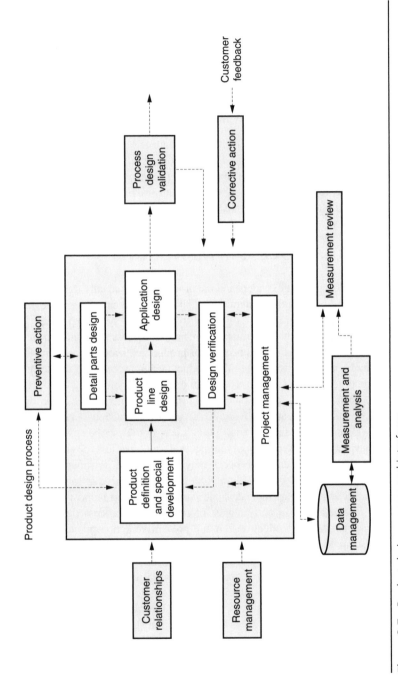

Figure 2.7   Product design process and interfaces.

IMPROVING THE PROCESSES OF THE QUALITY MANAGEMENT SYSTEM

To fully understand process interactions it is also useful to review the requirements of clauses 8.1 and 8.5.1. Clause 8.1 requires the organization to plan the continual improvement of quality management system effectiveness. Improving of the effectiveness of the overall system is dependent upon improvements carried out at the process level and it is best to plan for these improvements in planning the process.

Clause 8.5.1 provides additional detail for the improvement processes required. It requires that improvement be facilitated through the use of the quality policy, quality objectives, audit results, analysis of data, corrective and preventive actions, and management review. As we have seen, the processes of the quality management system should be directly related to the quality objectives. Analysis of data should include analysis of process performance and trends. As problems, nonconformities, or other undesirable conditions are identified during measurement, control, and analysis, they should be addressed through corrective action. Likewise, when potential problems are identified, preventive actions should be considered and implemented if they are appropriate.

THE KEY PROCESSES CONCEPT

Many organizations identify certain processes as *key processes* because those processes are the ones critical to achieving the organization's business goals and objectives. This concept is not found in ISO 9001:2000 but it is a useful one to use in managing a process-based quality management system focused on achieving results. While some of these processes may not be considered to be part of the quality management system, many often are. When this concept is used, it is generally these key processes on which the organization focuses its monitoring and measurement activities. It is always important to know which processes of the quality management system are important for achieving the organization's quality objectives, and these processes should be included in the organization's overall list of key processes. This concept often includes appointment of process champions or process owners for each key process.

PROCESS CHAMPIONS AND PROCESS OWNERS

Some organizations designate individuals to serve as process "owners" or "champions." A *process champion* is generally a member of the organization's top management who has interest in promoting the control and improvement of a specific process. A *process owner* is generally the head of one of the key functions involved in the actual operation of the process and is responsible for ensuring that the process is understood, documented, implemented, controlled, and improved. In some organizations the owner may be a department manager while the champion is a vice president. Other organizations make no distinction between owner and champion. In any case, having owners and/or champions for each key quality management system process can be an effective means to ensure that quality objectives are actually met. Where owners and champions exist, the audit boss should build excellent relationships with them to promote the use of the audit process as a key input to improving processes.

THE PROCESSES FOR PRODUCT REALIZATION

The previous discussion relates to the processes of the quality management system in general. Clause 7.1 deals more narrowly with the system's core processes for product realization. The processes for product realization include:

- Customer communications (clause 7.2)
- Design and development of the product (clause 7.3)
- Purchasing activities (clause 7.4)
- Production and service provision (clause 7.5)
- Control of monitoring and measuring devices (clause 7.6)

Clause 7.5.1 of ISO 9001:2000 provides more detailed requirements for control of those processes that focus on actual production of product or delivery of service. The requirements for planning product realization are similar to but a bit more specific than those of clause 4.1. In general, product realization planning is different from planning the quality management system. It relates to specific products and product lines, and to the family of processes used to design, develop, and produce products and services. Let's look at two examples:

- A single organization may have one quality management system but several sets of processes for product realization. Each of those separate product realization processes may be described in a document called a "quality plan." The distinction between planning the processes for product realization and the broader planning of the quality management system is very clear in such organizations.

- Alternatively, many organizations have single products or a single set of product realization processes. In such cases, the distinction between the quality management system processes and the processes for product realization may be quite blurred.

In either case, the product realization processes must be planned, implemented, and improved. Product realization planning needs to consider many things. These include the quality objectives for the product, the need to establish processes, the need for documents, provision for verification and validation for product design and development, and the need to provide monitoring activities specific to the product. As with the processes of the quality management system, it is important to understand the suppliers, inputs, activities, outputs, and customers for each process. Each product realization process should be monitored, and those important to meeting customer requirements and quality objectives should also be measured and analyzed. It is especially important to identify appropriate statistical methods to be used in control and improvement of the processes for product and service provision.

ISO 9001:1994 required that processes related to making products and delivering services be operated under controlled conditions. Specifically, Clause 4.9 of ISO 9001:1994 required organizations to:

. . . Identify and plan the production, installation, and servicing processes which directly affect quality and shall ensure that these processes are carried out under controlled conditions. . . .

The 1987 and 1994 versions of ISO 9001 used a procedural approach, putting procedural requirements on activities and functions. Except for clause 4.9, the 1994 standard did not directly address processes of the system. It did not directly connect the process of the system to quality objectives or relate the process approach with the system approach to management. ISO 9001:2000 recognizes that the entire system is made up of interrelated processes, so in addition to consideration of the processes for product realization (see clause 7.1), we must identify and manage the processes for the whole system. For many organizations, this will not prove to be a major change. If an organization has used flowcharts or process maps and has developed a process emphasis, then it is certainly possible that the new standard would require no difference in approach.

SUMMARY

The process approach requires clear deployment of the organization's quality objectives, clear understanding of the processes needed to meet those objectives, and the effective measurement and implementation of those processes. While such tools as process mapping, flowcharting, and statistical analysis are useful, measurement against properly established quality objectives is the most critical part of the approach.

A more extensive discussion of these concepts and their relationship to quality management system documentation can be found in chapters 2, 5, and 12 of *The ASQ ISO 9000:2000 Handbook* (Cianfrani et al.).

Since achieving quality objectives and meeting customer requirements is dependent on the processes of the quality management system, it follows that the audit program should focus on those processes as well. Auditing is a key means for determining whether these processes have been effectively implemented and for identifying opportunities for further process improvements. Auditing a process-based quality management system is the subject of the next chapter.

3

Auditing the Process-Based Quality Management System

ISO 9001:2000 introduces little change in the requirements for conducting internal audits. On the other hand, the process approach does offer the opportunity to audit processes as they flow through the functions of an organization. It also offers the opportunity to test the effectiveness of process interactions. This approach may prove to be a value-added activity. It has been said that while the 1994 version of ISO 9001 required "system audits," ISO 9001:2000 requires "process audits." However, the concept "process audit" is not defined in ISO 9000:2000 nor is the term "process audit" used in ISO 9001:2000. Do not be confused; auditors must still determine if the *system* is effectively implemented and maintained and if it meets the requirements of ISO 9001. Quality management system audits are still system audits! We will discuss true process auditing later in this chapter.

But wait a minute! ISO 9001:2000 requires that organizations use the process approach to developing, managing, and improving quality management systems. And shouldn't audits validate that the process approach itself has indeed been effectively implemented? Of course they should. It is hard to imagine how the application of the process approach can be audited without looking at the processes of the system. For many organizations this is not really new but for others it may mean major changes in auditing practices.

Interrelated processes are a fundamental part of any QMS and should be taken into account during audit planning. A more effective audit may be performed by taking the processes into account than by not, even though this is not a requirement of ISO 9001:2000. This may be done by auditing the processes of the system to ensure those processes meet the requirements of ISO 9001 and the organization's objectives. Auditing of the processes may be done function by function (for example, auditing all the processes that flow through a department or function) or by cross-functional auditing of each process. Process inputs and outputs should be considered as well as the organization's methods for monitoring and measuring the processes. Process measures and targets for key processes should be linked to the organization's quality objectives. Taking the processes into account means that you should consider a number of aspects related to each process. Let's look back at Figure 2.6 and discuss it in terms of auditing.

• *Outputs and customers.* Determine whether the internal and external customers of the process have been identified, if output requirements are clearly understood, and if the organization has defined the means to measure conformance to internal and external customer requirements.

• *Results.* Determine whether the results of the process meet internal objectives. This may be the most significant change that organizations should consider in auditing to ISO 9001:2000. Both the audit system and the auditors themselves should focus on evaluating whether process results meet objectives. One way to address this is to routinely provide a means for auditors to review process results prior to starting an audit of a process. This means that the audit boss should put in place mechanisms to ensure the data needed to make this determination are available prior to the start of an audit.

• *Inputs and suppliers.* Determine whether the suppliers to the process have been identified. These will be primarily internal suppliers. Determine whether the means to measure the suppliers' inputs against process requirements are known. Determine if these inputs are measured, and if they meet requirements.

• *Resources.* Resources must be provided to conduct the activities of the process. Resources include process equipment, information, people, and anything else that may be necessary to ensure effective operation of the process.

• *Controls.* The processes must operate under controlled conditions. This requires that specific means to control each process need to be provided, including appropriate documented requirements, measurement, monitoring, use of appropriate documented work instructions, and means for verification that requirements are met.

• *Process validation.* For production processes that require it, determine whether validation requirements have been established and met. In many organizations, process validation is *required* only for those processes where the results cannot be verified after product has been produced. On the other hand, there is a growing recognition that these verification activities can be eliminated or reduced if the process has a very high demonstrated capability and process controls are in place to ensure the process remains stable and in a state of control. This means that, in effect, the number of processes that are "validated" tends to be growing.

• *Competence of personnel.* Determine whether methods are in place to ensure that the personnel are competent. Competency includes both abilities and skills. Abilities come from physical and mental character-istics, and to an extent from education. Skills usually come from training and practice.

• *Monitoring and measurement of product.* Determine whether product verification requirements are being met. This may include the monitoring by operators of product characteristics by visual observation. It may involve automated monitoring equipment. It can also involve the taking of measurements. Where equipment is used in this monitoring, it should be controlled. In cases where measurement equipment is required, it must be calibrated and suitable for the measurements to be performed. (See discussion following for the difference between monitoring and measuring.)

• *Process monitoring and measurement.* Determine whether the meth-ods to monitor and (if required) measure process performance have been established and implemented. These activities should result in actions to correct any process problems and ensure that a state of control is main-tained. They may also result in actions to improve the process and its inter-actions with other processes.

• *Interactions with other processes.* Determine whether the relation-ships between the process or processes being examined and the other processes of the quality management system are properly understood and functioning effectively. Refer back to Figure 2.7. It can be seen that an audi-tor assigned to audit the "product design" process should consider the inter-actions of that process with a number of other processes. These include customer relationships, process design validation, resource management, data management, measurement and analysis, management review, correc-tive action, and preventive action.

• *Feedback from other processes and customers.* Determine whether a mechanism has been established to obtain and use feedback from internal and external customers of the process. Such feedback can result in actions to improve process performance or process outputs.

• *Process improvement.* Determine whether methods have been defined and implemented to improve the process. These activities may include some of the items discussed previously or other actions. It is important to remember that it is not necessary for the organization to improve every process all of the time. Organizations should be focusing on the processes that are important to meeting their quality objectives and to meeting internal and external customer requirements. When processes are performing well (meeting internal objectives and customer requirements), it may be best to expend improvement efforts on other processes. On the other hand, if a process is not meeting either customer requirements or internal objectives, there certainly should be improvement activities underway.

MONITORING VERSUS MEASUREMENT

There is an intended distinction between these two terms. *Monitoring* is a general term implying oversight over time. It can involve normal process observation by workers, daily supervision by managers, or the taking of process readings over time. It can involve automated alarms and other monitoring devices. Monitoring does not necessarily involve determination of numerical values. *Measurement* involves the actual determination of a value. It implies use of some measuring device to determine the numerical value of a product characteristic or process parameter at a given time.

QUALITY MANAGEMENT SYSTEM

Figure 3.1 shows a quality management system driven by top management and focused on meeting objectives and customer requirements. This system is process based and centered on measurements aligned with the quality objectives. Auditors should evaluate the extent to which these characteristics are evident in any process.

RELATIONSHIP OF DOCUMENTATION TO THE PROCESS APPROACH

It has already been pointed out that ISO 9001:2000 has streamlined documentation requirements. Prior editions of ISO 9001 used the "documentation approach" to quality management systems while ISO 9001:2000 relies much more heavily on the "process approach." *The idea is that it is far more important to manage the processes of the system than it is to ensure that there is a document for every requirement.* The processes should be operating under controlled conditions so that they consistently meet requirements

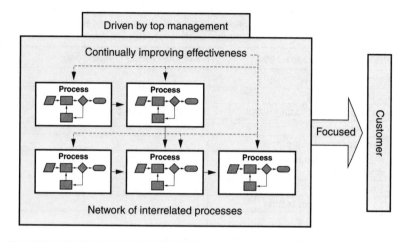

Figure 3.1   The quality management system: customer-focused, continually improving, and driven by top management.

and achieve planned results. Documentation may be of great assistance in providing such a state of control but it is not the only thing that is important. The documents required in ISO 9001:2000 may be grouped into four types:

• *Policy, objectives, and system description.* This includes the documented statement of quality policy and the documented quality objectives. It also includes the quality manual that describes how the various processes of the quality management system interact.

• *Process documents.* These include the six documented procedures specifically required by ISO 9001:2000. The requirements for documented procedures in ISO 9001:2000 are shown in Table 3.1, which compares these requirements to those of ISO 9001:1994. The requirements also include any other documents needed to ensure the effective planning, operation, and control of the processes. These other documents may include additional documented procedures, flowcharts of processes, organization charts, and anything else the organization may determine to be necessary or desirable.

• *Work instructions.* These are documents that describe how to perform specific activities related to product production and service provision. They may also give specific product characteristics, such as batch composition or software code module inputs. Clause 7.5.1 requires that these instructions be provided as appropriate to the circumstances. This means work instructions must exist if they are necessary to ensure that the process will be carried out under controlled conditions.

Table 3.1 ISO 9001:2000 requirements for documented procedures compared to similar requirements from ISO 9001:1994.

ANSI/ISO/ASQC Q9001-1994	ANSI/ISO/ASQ Q9001-2000
4.3.1 Contract review	
4.4.1 Design control	
4.5.6 Document and data control	4.2.3 Control of documents
4.6.1 Purchasing	
4.7 Customer supplied product	
4.8 Product identification and traceability	
4.9 Process control	
4.10.1 Inspection and testing	
4.11.1 Control of measuring and test equipment	
4.12 Inspection and test status	
4.13.1 Control of nonconforming product	8.3 Control of nonconforming product
4.14.1 Corrective and preventive action	8.5.2 Corrective action
	8.5.3 Preventive action
4.15.1 Handling, storage, packaging, preservation, and delivery of product	
4.16 Control of quality records	4.2.4 Control of records
4.17 Internal quality audits	8.2.2 Internal audits
4.18 Training	
4.19 Servicing	
4.20 Statistical techniques	

• *Records.* Records are required by ISO 9001:2000 to demonstrate that requirements have been met. Certain clauses of ISO 9001:2000 have their own specific requirements for records, and clauses 7.1 and 7.5.1 require that the organization plan the records to be developed during the product realization processes. Records are a key item for auditors. They are one of the most significant things auditors must review.

EXTENT OF DOCUMENTATION

Note 2 of clause 4.1 of ISO 9001:2000 explains that the extent of the documentation should be dependent upon the complexity of the processes in the organization, the complexity of the interactions between those processes, the size of the organization, and the competence of the personnel. It is not the auditor's job to determine the extent of documentation. This means that auditors may be faced with situations where there is not a documented procedure for a process they are auditing.

Figure 3.2 lists a few of the customer-related processes of an organization and illustrates a thought process for deciding if there is a need for a documented procedure. In the example, design validation is a very important process for the organization because it is the process that determines if customers will buy the product. The validation is done by a small group of people using focus-group techniques. The group is highly competent and the process is quite simple. The organization has elected to have no documented procedure for their design validation process. On the other hand, if the customer-related processes shown in Figure 3.2 are complex because of multiple distribution channels for the product and high personnel turnover (with lower overall competence levels) in the responsible functions, then documented procedures may be a necessity.

ISO 9001:2000 tends to emphasize the use of documentation as an element in controlling processes. The auditor may be faced with situations where the organization has chosen to rely on other control techniques and there are no (or very limited) written documents specifying how the process is to be operated.

Such cases should not be an impediment to auditing. It is not the auditor's job to merely determine if there is a documented procedure for an

> This organization has identified three key customer-related processes and considers documented procedures to be needed for two of them

Customer-Related Processes

Process	Documented Procedure Required by 9001?	Personnel Competence	Process and Interaction Complexity	Organization Size	Documented Procedure Needed?
Customer communication	No	Average	High	Small	Yes
Warranty	No	Average	Moderate	Small	Yes
Design validation	No	High	Low	Small	No

Figure 3.2   Decision-making process for determining the need for documented procedures.

operation and to verify that the people involved in the process are meeting the requirements of that documented procedure. That would be a very simplistic view of an audit. In such cases, the auditor must still start with the process results, verify that the process's inputs and outputs are meeting requirements, and that the activities are achieving required process outputs. Process outcomes should meet requirements. There should be close alignment between operators as to what is required and how to perform the activities. Similarly, there should be close alignment between the operators and their leaders as to what the requirements are.

SYSTEM AUDITS VERSUS PROCESS AUDITS

We mentioned earlier in this chapter that the audits required by ISO 9001:2000 are really quality management *system* audits and not "process" audits. We make this distinction because we have seen a good deal of confusion on this point. Let's describe the difference:

• *Process audit.* This type of audit is a short (usually a matter of hours) but intense analysis of a single process for creating a product (for example, a part, a purchase order, a calibration), subassembly, or product characteristic. Since it is tightly focused on a single process, such as welding, turning, cooking, mail sorting, and so on, it does not look at process interactions or process results except as they directly affect the characteristic under study. Its purpose is narrow: determining if the process is effectively (and perhaps efficiently) meeting requirements. True process audits have their place in the battery of audit tools. They *should* be used particularly for processes that depend upon operator skills or other sources of inherently high variability. They are appropriate for analyzing automated production processes as well. Process audits require understanding the process in minute detail, and attempting to use them for auditing quality management systems processes is not an effective use of resources. In a quality management system scenario, use of the technique can result in not seeing the forest for the trees! Significant overall issues can be missed while minute details are emphasized, thus defeating the very purpose of the system audit.

• *System audit.* This is a much broader evaluation and its purpose is to ensure that the overall system is effective in meeting its objectives, the organization's own internal system requirements, and ISO 9001:2000. Even though an individual internal quality management system audit may focus on a single process such as "product design," its purpose is much broader than the process audit. Its purpose is to evaluate how effectively the overall quality management system is implemented. It is a much higher-level activity than a process audit and covers much more territory but is not as detailed.

The third edition of *Quality Audits for Improved Performance* by Dennis R. Arter contains a comprehensive discussion of the different audit types.

ALTERNATIVE STRATEGIES FOR ISO 9001:2000 AUDIT PROGRAMS

There are certainly several ways an organization can structure a quality audit program to meet the internal audit requirement of ISO 9001:2000. One way would be to simply divide the standard into a number of its basic process-related parts and audit each of these without regard to the organization's own processes, organization, and workflows. This is certainly possible and might meet the requirements for an audit program, but it certainly is not efficient; and, since it tends to ignore the organization's processes, it is not likely to prove very effective in stimulating performance improvements. Let's look at other alternatives:

• *Audit the processes.* Structure the audits around the major management, support, and product realization processes of the quality management system as they are defined in the quality manual. This approach is often called a *horizontal audit.* Since processes tend to flow through the functions of the organization, this approach would cover the major functions as well as the interfaces between the functions and the processes. It may, however, have the disadvantage of missing many of the interactions between the key processes of the system, although this disadvantage can be overcome with careful audit designs. While it is probably impossible to design a system that audits all of the processes, each major process can be covered to sufficient levels of detail to ensure compliance with ISO 9001:2000.

• *Audit the functions.* Structure the audits around the major organizational functions. Include in each of these audits all the processes for which the function being audited has any responsibility. This approach is often called a *vertical audit.* It is likely to be a somewhat better approach overall than the first. It has the advantage of covering all of the key processes and their interfaces within the function being audited. If process "handoffs" to and from the function are considered, it also provides a window on problems at functional boundaries. It is fairly efficient because each function need be visited only once per audit cycle.

In actual practice, audit programs may use a combination of these approaches. This provides flexibility. Vertical audits can be used for functional areas that have responsibility for major parts of the overall system, as may be true for "design engineering," "purchasing," or the "production department." For these major functions, it may be more efficient and effective to conduct a single audit that encompasses all processes for which they have responsibilities. Other processes may have responsibilities so spread out that a horizontal, cross-functional audit of the process is best. As the organizational structure changes over time and the quality management system matures, the combination approach provides the flexibility to change to meet emerging needs. For example, if several functions seem to have difficulties with a particular cross-functional process that has been audited during prior functional audits, perhaps the next audit cycle should include a cross-functional audit of that process.

SUMMARY

Although the requirements for conducting audits have not changed, we strongly recommend that internal audits focus on outputs, improvement, customer satisfaction, and alignment with other areas of the organization. Audit planning should consider all the requirements of all the clauses in ISO 9001:2000 that apply to the process or activity being audited. This approach to internal audit planning and implementation will, we believe, yield the best return on the internal auditing investment.

One of the basic ideas of the process-based quality management system is that activities are managed together with resources under a state of control. When evaluating quality management systems, there are a number of questions that are important to ask about every process being evaluated in every audit:

- Is the process identified and appropriately described?

- Are responsibilities assigned?

- Are process controls in place?

- Are procedures (documented or not) implemented and maintained?

- Are the requirements clearly specified and understood?

- Is the process monitored (and if required, measured) as appropriate?

- Is the process effective in achieving the required results?

- Is the process continually improved?

Additional questions that may be asked for each process in audits for performance improvement:

- Is the process meeting all of its performance objectives?

- Does the process pose significant risks of future process problems or product nonconformities?

- Are there redundant or unnecessary activities?

- Can this process or some of its activities be combined with other processes for increased effectiveness or efficiency?

The collective answers to the above questions determine the outcome of the evaluation.

4

Audit Objectives: Meeting Requirements and Performance Improvement

A udits are conducted for a variety of reasons. They have different purposes or objectives. Part III, chapter 8 will address determination of audit objectives in some detail. The purpose of this chapter is to discuss the basic distinction between audits that focus only on whether requirements of ISO 9001:2000 and the internal quality management system are being met and those that have determination of opportunities for improvement of the organization's performance as an objective. Dennis R. Arter discusses the distinction between compliance audits and performance audits in detail in the third edition of *Quality Audits for Improved Performance*. This chapter discusses these two concepts as they apply to auditing a process-based quality management system developed to meet the requirements of ISO 9001:2000.

Understanding this distinction is important because it can drive audit planning, the assignment of auditors, and the types of questions they ask. Let's first dispose of the assumption that audits focusing only on meeting requirements are somehow inferior to those also looking for improvement opportunities.

CONCEPTS RELATED TO AUDITING TO VERIFY THAT REQUIREMENTS ARE BEING MET

Conformity of the quality management system to its requirements is crucial to achieving a foundation from which improvements can spring. Conformity assessment (registration) audits focus on whether the requirements of ISO 9001:2000 are being met. Customer audits of suppliers focus on conformity to the customer's requirements. Internal audits are used to verify that the organization is meeting the ISO 9001:2000 requirements as well as the organization's own internal requirements. It is necessary to improve the system's effectiveness in meeting those requirements. In fact, it is common for the internal quality audit program to contribute to improving system effectiveness for a number of years simply by identifying instances where the system has broken down or is not being followed. And even after the quality management system has matured it is useful to use audits to ensure ongoing system effectiveness. Let's look at the characteristics of audits that are focused only on determining whether the system meets the requirements of ISO 9001:2000 and the organization's own planned arrangements:

• *Audit criteria.* When the audit objective is to examine whether the requirements of ISO 9001:2000 are being met, the criteria are taken as the fixed requirements of the standard and of the quality management system documents. The criteria may be considered as minimums to be met or exceeded but those minimum requirements are a given.

• *Audit techniques.* In this type of audit the majority of the audit time is expended in asking questions related to, and reviewing records to substantiate fulfillment of requirements. Audit questions tend to relate to what is being accomplished, how it is being accomplished, and whether the activities are conducted as required. Note that the focus is on the required *activities.*

• *Expected audit output.* The expected result of this type of internal audit is stable, consistent process operations. The output of such audits is either good (statements that a process meets requirements and the existence of evidence to support that conclusion) or findings that requirements are not being met (again with supporting evidence).

• *Resulting actions.* These audits focus on maintaining stability so the resulting actions either maintain good performance or return performance to a stable state that meets the requirements. The most common result is a request for corrective action to address nonconformity to requirements.

CONCEPTS RELATED TO AUDITING FOR IMPROVED PERFORMANCE

Understanding and meeting requirements, our own and the customers', is critical. There is nothing wrong with audits to ensure that our processes accomplish this. But is it sufficient to simply meet minimum requirements? In times when competitors constantly challenge and owners demand real improvements this may not be sufficient. More and more, top managers are seeking every opportunity to get better, to more effectively meet customer needs, and to more efficiently carry out operations.

If such circumstances exist for your organization, it may be time to include the identification of performance improvement opportunities in the audit program. Lets look at some of the characteristics of audits that include performance improvement as an objective:

• *Audit criteria.* Auditing for performance improvement implies that the level of desired performance has been specified in some performance criteria. It should be those performance criteria that form the basis auditors will use to define performance gaps. Criteria used in audits for performance improvement are not assumed to be unchangeable, fixed requirements. *In these audits it is at least as important to challenge the requirements themselves as it is to determine whether the requirements are being met.*

• *Audit techniques.* In this type of audit, at least some of the time is spent examining whether results meet expected performance requirements and on why those performance criteria are or are not being met. In conducting audits for performance improvement, it is also necessary to ask questions about why activities are conducted as they are.

• *Expected audit output.* The expected results of performance audits include business performance improvements. This means that the audit outputs should include identification of best practices (when performance is very good), identification of gaps between current process performance and some possible improved level of performance (with evidence to support existence of the gap), and identification of major risks that are observed in the current process (with evidence and quantification of the risk).

• *Resulting actions.* Change is the basic activity that should be expected following each performance audit. In addition to corrective action, these changes can include basic process redesign, implementation of preventive action, or changes to required activities to meet performance objectives.

Figure 4.1 graphically illustrates some of the distinctions between these two types of audit processes. The distinction is not just theoretical. It affects audit planning, auditor selection, audit conduct, audit reporting, follow-up actions taken, and the type of results the audit program can achieve. It is absolutely essential that the audit boss, auditees, and auditors clearly understand whether performance improvement is one of the audit objectives.

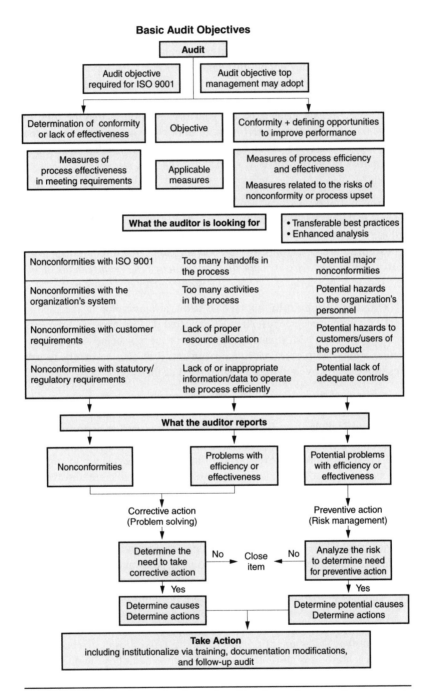

Figure 4.1 Auditing for conformity and auditing for performance improvement.

AUDITING FOR PERFORMANCE IMPROVEMENT AND CONSULTING

Auditors never provide advice on what actions should be taken to resolve issues or gaps. This should be obvious in audits that examine only whether requirements are being met. This principle is also important when audit objectives include performance improvement. Notice that in auditing for performance improvement, the audit process stops with clear identification of a potential risk or a gap in performance. It is appropriate to include data to substantiate the gap or risk, to quantify it, and to show the process activities that impact results. Auditors should not get involved in recommending the action to be taken. This work should be left to the auditee. Auditors may be requested to participate on problem-solving teams to address audit-defined issues. They are now contributing experts and consultants and no longer auditors. Depending on the level of input, this involvement on systems design may prevent the auditor from auditing those processes for a period of time. This "cooling off" is designed to maintain objectivity in the auditors as well as the audit program.

Part II

Audit Program Management

INTRODUCTION

Part I provided a broad overview of the basic elements of auditing, and specifically auditing ISO 9001:2000 based quality management systems. Part II describes general requirements for establishing and managing an efficient and effective internal audit program.

This section is divided into three chapters. Chapter 5 addresses the essential nature of the internal audit program from an administrative viewpoint and how it can be established, monitored, and measured to ensure it is meeting the objectives of the organization.

Chapter 6 provides insight into the selection and training of internal auditors, including expectations of their behavior and ethics. It also addresses the assessment and monitoring of auditor performance.

Chapter 7 discusses the use of the output of the internal audit process from the viewpoint of the organization. It considers how audit results can be reviewed, analyzed, and used collectively to enhance improvement and customer satisfaction initiatives in addition to the actions that are taken as a result of individual audit reports (individual audit reports are addressed in detail in Part III chapter 10). Chapter 7 considers questions such as "Are audit reports considered collectively?" and "Are the data analyzed to uncover trends or opportunities that may not be obvious when initially reported in individual reports?"

Together these three chapters describe how to implement an effective internal audit program in an organization.

5

The Internal Audit Program

CHARTERING OF THE INTERNAL AUDIT PROGRAM

There are many reasons to perform internal quality audits. On one end of the scale, there could be recognition by senior managers in the organization of the importance of:

- Having confidence that processes are operating in accordance with defined and planned arrangements

- Systematically pursuing opportunities for improvement

This is similar to the desire of top management to conduct financial audits that provide confidence to all stakeholders that transactions are being conducted in accordance with generally accepted accounting principles (GAAP).

Enlightened top management might even recognize that internal quality auditing can be valuable to an organization because it focuses on ensuring customer satisfaction at the present time and into the future, and not just on assessing past performance.

Alternatively (and at the other end of the motivation scale), top management might recognize that an internal quality audit process is required by clause 8.2.2 of ISO 9001:2000 and authorize internal quality audits solely to meet ISO requirements.

However it is initiated and whatever the motivation, *top management has the responsibility to charter the internal audit process.* In chartering the audit process, top management must direct that it be implemented and must assign the necessary resources to ensure effective implementation.

DECISIONS THAT SHOULD BE MADE DURING THE CHARTERING PROCESS

 When chartering the internal audit program, there are decisions that need to be made in the areas of basic objectives, the relationship of the quality auditing process to other assessment activities, and resource requirements.

Basic Audit Program Objectives

 An internal audit may be performed for two basic reasons: compliance assurance or performance improvement. This distinction was discussed in chapter 4 of Part I. Top management will always have a need to know how well the organization complies with internal and external requirements. If the organization is in a regulated market (for example, medical device manufacturing), compliance with regulations is mandatory (for example, FDA, ISO 13485).

The organization may also decide to audit for both compliance assurance and performance improvement. We believe this second approach is more desirable.

Integration, or Not, with Other Audit Programs

Audit programs can benefit other areas besides quality. Certainly most organizations require financial audits; environmental audits and health and safety audits are becoming increasingly common. Top management should address how it will meet all these audit demands. An organization can have separate internal quality; environmental, occupational health, and safety (EHS); operations; and financial audit programs. Or EHS and quality auditing can be integrated, with operations and financial audits being kept separate. Or all auditing can be assigned to one internal audit group that has full-time competent staff dedicated to auditing all required operations and processes. This last approach is quite difficult to successfully implement. The combination of QMS and EHS auditing is becoming more common.

Provision of Resources

The provision of resources is a top management responsibility that should not be treated casually. Areas that require management deliberation and decisions include:

- Assignment of an "audit boss" (called *audit program management* in the ISO 19011:2000 standard). This could be a full-time job for an audit process administrator, an audit coordinator, a director of internal audit, or someone with a similar title. Or, audit boss responsibilities may be assigned to a quality director, quality manager, or even a designated management representative (see paragraph 5.5.2 of ISO 9001:2000).

- Allocation of time for the audit boss to plan, administer, evaluate, and improve the internal audit process.

- Provision of staff to perform internal audits as directed by the audit boss.

- Provision of time for auditees to participate by answering questions and responding to auditors' requests for information and data.

- Provision of equipment, space, and payroll budgets to support the audit staff.

- Provision of resources to train and maintain the competence of internal auditors.

- Commitment of top management and others to consider, and use as appropriate, the output of the internal audit process.

DISSEMINATING THE INTERNAL AUDIT CHARTER

Top management should clearly and unequivocally communicate the relevance and importance of internal auditing to the organization as an important strategy and tactic for achieving customer satisfaction and operational excellence. This can be accomplished through corporate policy statements, e-mail and newsletter communications to employees, positioning the audit boss prominently in the organizational hierarchy, and by requiring establishment and documentation (for example, procedures) of a robust audit process. Top management should also reinforce the importance of internal auditing by being directly involved in audit planning and by reviewing results. They should also take action when performance gaps exist. Management can lead by example and by being involved.

Top management also needs to be aware of and address the ISO 9001:2000 requirements for quality management system planning (clauses 4.1 and 5.4.2) and quality objectives (clause 5.4.1) when structuring, chartering, and initiating the quality audit program. The internal quality audit process does not exist in a vacuum. It is just one element of the quality management system, although some argue that it is one of the three most vital elements (along with management review and corrective action).

Finally, the basic structure and functioning of the audit program should be reviewed formally at least annually to ensure that it is still appropriate and to make necessary changes. The management review process is a reasonable venue for such a periodic review.

ESTABLISHING AN INTERNAL AUDIT PROCESS

Once top management has decided that the organization shall implement an internal audit process, has anointed (or at least appointed) an audit boss, and has committed resources to this activity, it is logical to develop detailed audit program objectives and processes. It is particularly important to carefully consider the objectives of the audit program since these objectives will provide the criteria for evaluating, analyzing, and improving the audit program.

The development of an audit program should be similar to the development of any other process of the quality management system, or, for that matter, to the development of any product. In simple terms, the activities are:

1. Define the requirements for the audit program including consideration of all of the areas discussed above and in part I (for example, this could be in the form of a flowchart, a process map, or a requirements specification).

2. Plan the program to meet the objectives (refer to ISO 9001:2000 clause 5.4.2).

3. Develop the program (clause 7.3 may be helpful here, especially 7.3.4—design review).

4. Ensure that the program meets the defined requirements and is consistent with policy and objectives.

5. Verify that the process as developed meets the defined requirements.

6. Validate the process by at least reviewing it with top management to ensure that it meets their needs.

PREPARING AN INTERNAL AUDIT PROCEDURE

Clause 8.2.2 of ISO 9001:2000 requires "the responsibilities and require- ments for planning and conducting (internal) audits, and for reporting results and maintaining records (see ISO 9001:2000 clause 4.2.4), shall be defined in a documented procedure."

 After the internal audit processes have been developed and approved by top management, it is time to create the procedure required by ISO 9001:2000 clause 8.2.2. This procedure should address at least the following elements:

- Defining objectives of the overall internal audit program. (The purpose and scope of individual audits will be defined as part of the audit preparation steps, discussed in Part III, chapter 8.)

- Making the schedule of the audits to be performed, including selection of the processes, areas, and functions to be audited.

- Disseminating an annual plan of what to audit.

- Selecting auditors and addressing restrictions on who can audit what.

- Identifying responsibilities for planning and conducting audits and reporting results.

- Ensuring that corrective action and follow-up methods are defined.

The internal audit procedure does not have to be long or complex. It should be adequate to ensure the administration of an effective internal audit program. This procedure is generally "owned" by the audit boss. Figure 5.1 is an example of a simple internal audit procedure.

ANNUAL AUDIT PLANNING AND SCHEDULING

Selection of the processes/areas to be audited is typically made by the audit boss based on their importance to the organization, past performance, and the availability of competent auditors.

Sample Internal Audit Procedure (ISO 9001:2000 Clause 8.2.2)

1.0 Purpose:

To provide direction for internal quality auditing.

2.0 Scope:

Applies to all functional departments and activities within the organization, with the exception of accounting and legal.

3.0 Reference Documentation:

ISO 9001:2000, clause 8.2.2
ISO 19011:2000 (*Guidelines for quality and/or environmental management systems auditing*)
Quality Policy Manual and Quality Objectives

4.0 Requirements:

The management representative shall prepare an annual audit schedule, showing audits to be performed throughout the year. The schedule shall be presented to the plant manager for review and approval and distributed to all affected departments by December 15. The schedule shall be reviewed quarterly for appropriateness. Internal audits shall be conducted on a periodic basis, with all aspects of the quality management system being audited within a three-year period.

The management representative shall maintain a list of qualified personnel to conduct internal audits. The management representative shall assure that personnel assigned to perform internal audits are competent, impartial, and objective. Auditors may not audit their own work or methods they have developed within the past year.

A team of one or more qualified auditors shall conduct individual audits. Each audit shall have an audit plan, approved by the management representative prior to commencing the data gathering and interviews. The plan shall be sent to the affected parties no later than one week prior to the opening meeting. Upon completion of each audit, a report shall be prepared and presented to the management

Figure 5.1   Example of a simple audit program procedure.   *Continued*

Continued

representative within two working days for distribution. Adverse audit findings, if any, shall be captured on corrective action request forms.

The disposition of any corrective action requests as the result of an internal audit shall follow the corrective action procedure.

The management representative shall review all internal audit reports and shall analyze them for trends and opportunities for improvement and shall report the results of this analysis to senior management at least once a quarter.

Figure 5.1 Example of a simple audit program procedure.

Area Schedule	Product Design & Development	Corrective Action	Product Realization Process #1	Product Realization Process #2	Product Realization Process #3	Etc. →
1Q	Auditor 1		Auditor 7			
2Q		Audit Team 2		Auditor 12		
3Q					Audit Team 3	
4Q		Audit Team 4				

Figure 5.2 Annual audit schedule.

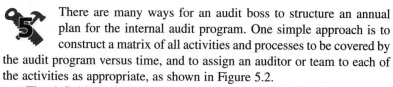

There are many ways for an audit boss to structure an annual plan for the internal audit program. One simple approach is to construct a matrix of all activities and processes to be covered by the audit program versus time, and to assign an auditor or team to each of the activities as appropriate, as shown in Figure 5.2.

The definition of the audit criteria, the methods to be used, and the scope of individual audits are typically stated in an *audit plan* that is prepared prior to each audit. (See Part III, chapter 8 for more information on the audit plan.)

MAINTENANCE OF THE
AUDIT SCHEDULE

The audit boss should constantly assess the progress of the audits against the annual schedule and make modifications as appropriate. For example, if several customer complaints are received by phone for a particular product, the audit boss could initiate a special audit of processes related to that product. Similarly, if a major restructuring occurs, the audit boss could direct audit attention to those areas most likely to be affected by the restructuring to ensure the continuing integrity of the quality management system throughout the organization. Common practice is to require a quarterly review of the audit schedule to make sure it remains relevant to the organization's needs.

ASSIGNMENT OF AUDITORS

One important responsibility of the audit boss is the selection and assignment of auditors. The audit boss must understand the nature of the audits to be performed (for example, if there is unique process knowledge required) and have a feel for the personalities of individuals to maximize the likelihood for a successful audit experience. If a team will conduct an audit, the audit boss must ensure that the team as a whole has the competence, skills, and specific product and process knowledge to successfully complete an assigned audit.

The audit boss also must provide oversight in the assignment of auditors to assure that auditors provide impartial and objective assessment of the audited process or function. One approach is for the audit boss to appoint a team leader and allow the team leader to gather team members from the rest of the organization. However, the audit boss is still accountable to top management for the overall quality of all auditors on a team.

MONITORING AND MEASURING THE
INTERNAL AUDIT PROCESS

Similar to other processes of the quality management system, the internal audit process requires at least monitoring and perhaps measurement. The audit boss should identify key indicators of performance of the audit processes and institute appropriate monitoring and/or measurement of these processes. Here are some possible metrics:

- Percentage of audits started on time

- Number of complaints regarding auditor performance

- Number of disputed audit findings

- Percentage of audit plans accepted with no modifications

- Percentage of audit reports completed on time (for example, within *x* days of audit)

- Percentage of audit reports accepted by audit boss on first pass (complete and accurate)

- Time period between the exit meeting and delivery of the written (paper or e-mail) report

- Number of overdue responses to corrective action requests generated from adverse audit findings

- Number of times the auditee disagrees with the conclusions of the audit report or its individual adverse findings

- Number of accepted recommendations for improvement

- Turnover of the audit staff

As with every process, monitoring performance will keep it stable and perhaps result in process improvement. The audit boss should review and analyze data generated from monitoring and measurement of the internal audit process and use the results for improvement.

In the areas of monitoring, measuring, and improving the internal audit process, there are at least three responsibilities that the audit boss should discharge:

- Ensuring coherent input is provided to the management review process

- Ensuring analysis of all audit reports collectively to uncover trends or opportunities for improvement that are not apparent in the individual reports

- Seeking input from internal customers and other stakeholders regarding audit process effectiveness

Evidence of analysis of the consolidated data provided by the audit reports and monitoring of the audit processes are indicators of an effective internal audit program. The audit boss needs to institutionalize these activities.

MANAGEMENT REVIEW

If the analysis and improvement mentioned previously are important, then providing coherent input to the management review process is vital. The organization makes a significant investment in its internal audit process. The return on this investment comes from three primary sources:

1. Elimination of the recurrence of nonconformities that were identified as a result of an audit.

2. Improvements that result from auditor–auditee interactions, such as auditor feedback to the auditee on process methods, or an auditor seeing a "best practice" in the area being audited that can be "ported" to other areas of the organization.

3. Action by top management to address generic or systemic issues (not individual corrective actions). These systemic issues are typically not resolvable at lower levels in the organization since they require investment of capital (human or financial, or both) to address such issues.

It is in this last area where the audit boss can have significant influence on the organization. Simply put, by superbly analyzing all aspects of internal audit performance and reporting to top management in language they understand, and by effective use of the management review process, the audit boss will ensure that the organization derives value for the investment made in internal auditing.

6

Auditors

To perform internal audits, an organization needs auditors. Where does it find such individuals? There are basically three approaches: (1) use contractors, (2) use full-time employees whose full-time job is auditing, or (3) use employees who perform audits on a part-time basis.

The first approach is to hire outsiders to perform most or all of the quality audit function. Contracted suppliers now perform payroll, maintenance, and even manufacturing. This is called outsourcing. Internal auditing may also be accomplished by outsourcing. This is especially useful for very small organizations (that is, less than 30 people), where everyone wears multiple hats. However, it has a potential for failure for several reasons including:

- Outside auditors have little or no interest in the success of the organization. They may act like "hired guns" or be seen as such.

- They typically have a modest, if not a steep, learning curve.

- They have limited ability to uncover opportunities for improvement.

However, if contractors are treated as employees and subjected to the same checks and balances as employee auditors, they can be cost-effective. Our advice here is, "If you contract your auditing to another firm, apply the same controls as you would to your own people." (See Table 6.1 for a comparison of the advantages and disadvantages of the various options for performing internal audits.)

Table 6.1 Sources of internal audit personnel.

Source	Advantages	Disadvantages
Outside— contractors	High competence in auditing techniques Audits may be performed more efficiently	Do not "know" organization Expensive No vested interest in organization
Inside— full-time	High competence Know company Know processes Vested interest	Expensive to maintain a dedicated audit staff Limited cross-fertilization across departments
Inside— part-time	Low cost Cross-fertilization Auditors are more aware of issues in their own areas	Not audit professionals Scheduling can be an issue

The more common approach is to create a cadre of internal auditors, either full- or part-time, from among the existing staff of the organization. There is certainly an investment that must be made in developing competence. Training must be provided and auditors must acquire experience, but this investment pays dividends in many ways over time. For example, at the very least these auditors will be able to self-audit and improve their own areas of influence. Also, through learning and communication, auditors can help to break down interdepartmental barriers. Finally, auditing can contribute to employee satisfaction by adding a degree of variety to a job that might be getting routine.

NUMBER OF AUDITORS

How many auditors does an organization require? The answer is a definitive "it depends." Let's consider a few hypothetical scenarios:

• *Scenario 1.* The audit boss has developed an annual audit plan that includes conducting 20 audits during the year that are each estimated to require one day on average to perform. For a one-day audit, it is reasonable to expect half a day to prepare for the audit and half a day to document the results. Therefore, the audit boss must ensure the availability of 40 days to satisfy this part of the audit plan. If the audit boss has full-time staff available (several quality engineers and quality auditors), it may simply be a matter of assigning the workload to staff and ensuring enough time is available to do auditing as well as other assigned duties. If part-time auditors will be used, and each auditor will be expected to perform no more than three audits per year, then the audit boss will need a pool of seven competent auditors who will be expected to dedicate a minimum of six days per year to performing audits. The audit boss would be well advised to have a slightly larger pool available, perhaps ten auditors, to allow for the inevitable scheduling conflicts that arise when utilizing part-time auditors.

• *Scenario 2.* Suppose the audit boss decides to limit the scope of some audits to approximately four hours and suppose these audits will be performed by individuals in the organization that have other full-time responsibilities. Further suppose that each audit requires two hours of preparation and two hours to write the report. Thus each audit will take approximately one working day. Further, suppose the audit boss decides that each auditor will be required to perform no more than three audits per year. If the audit boss identifies 30 narrow-scope audits to be performed during the year, there will be a requirement for a minimum of 10 trained auditors to complete these audits, and allowing for contingency, 12 would be a comfortable number.

A whole range of other scenarios is possible depending on the anticipated scope of the audits and whether audits are done individually or by a team. It is not uncommon to have a mix of auditors, some full-time and some part-time, as well as a mix of audit scopes, with some very narrowly-focused (for example, a specific manufacturing cell) and others more far-reaching (for example, the entire development process). The point is that the audit boss needs to ensure the availability of a sufficient number of competent auditors to implement the audit plan.

In addition to time to perform actual audits, the audit boss should anticipate training overhead of two or three days per auditor each year to maintain competence. See the discussion below on qualification of auditors for more details.

If part-time internal auditors are used, the audit boss needs to be sensitive to the time demands even though the benefits are substantial.

SELECTION OF AUDITORS

When seeking candidates for internal auditing, where would the audit boss look? The answer is easy—everywhere. Engineering personnel, IT project managers, financial auditors, and top management may all have the skills and demeanor to be very successful internal auditors. Experienced operators, lead technicians, facilitators, coordinators, analysts, and supervisors typically possess the process knowledge to perform internal audits. It also helps if top management makes a clear statement that internal auditing is important, that they are willing to make the investment necessary to ensure that the internal audit activity is staffed by the best and brightest personnel available, and that they consider auditing to be valuable experience for those with ambition for advancement and promotion.

 There are three basic requirements for any auditor or audit team member (remember that an audit team can be one or more auditors).

1. *Lack of vested interest.* Do they have the ability to see important clues?

2. *Technical knowledge of the processes and systems to be audited.* Do they know what the clues mean?

3. *Skills in the process of auditing, including planning, performing, and reporting.* Can they present their results in a meaningful way?

 Each auditor or team member need not have the same degree of competence in each of these three areas, but together, the team must possess all three.

A guideline of what to look for is more difficult, but the following checklist of characteristic qualifications may prove helpful to an audit boss when evaluating and selecting personnel to perform internal audits:

- *Inquisitive nature.* An individual who wonders how things work may make a good auditor.

- *Oral communication skills.* Auditors must have the ability to ask clear, coherent questions.

- *Listening skills.* Active listening is a requirement for a good auditor.

- *Project and time management skills.* Auditors need to manage their time and conduct audits in a logical manner.

- *Ability to get along with people.* Argumentative individuals generally do not make good auditors.

- *Writing skills.* Auditors need to be able to write coherent and compelling reports that engender action.

- *Organizational skills.* Auditors need to handle volumes of paper and information and quickly separate the important from the trivial.

- *Flexibility.* Willing to look at new approaches and understand benefits (and risks).

Part I, chapter 1 contained a discussion of audit principles and ethics. All these issues must be considered when evaluating the suitability of individuals to perform internal audits.

Selecting individuals with the skills, willingness, and capability to be competent internal auditors is indeed a challenge, but no different than making any other personnel decision. If the audit boss has a sound job specification and conducts thorough interviews, it should not be difficult to find an adequate staff of full-time or part-time internal auditors who, with appropriate training and supervision, will perform competently, and perhaps even superbly.

One other selection issue an audit boss needs to address is the selection of individuals to function as audit team leaders (sometimes called lead auditors). The selection and designation of audit leaders is an activity that deserves thoughtful contemplation by the audit boss. In addition to the competencies necessary to be an auditor, a leader needs to be experienced in handling matters such as the procedural aspects of auditing, conducting opening meetings, writing great reports and organizing and directing the work of individuals who may not report to the audit leader.

AUDITOR COMPETENCE

 A word about training and competence is appropriate here. As a minimum, any individual who will be conducting or leading internal audits should start as a trainee and be qualified by the audit boss before being permitted to conduct actual audits. The audit boss is responsible for assessing the competence of individuals who will be conducting internal audits. For some, a few hours of training on the mechanics of the internal auditing methodology of an organization may be adequate to ensure competence. For others, no amount of training would be adequate. There is a diversity of opinion regarding the minimum amount of training an internal auditor requires, and indeed, even if the amount of training should be a criterion for assessing competence. To provide a starting point, an organization could consider the following items when deciding what training and experience is necessary to ensure auditor competence:

- Formal training on ISO 9001:2000. Each auditor should have a good understanding of both the requirements of ISO 9001:2000 and the terminology used in ISO 9000:2000.

- Formal training on other requirements that are applicable to the organization. This would include government regulations for organizations producing regulated products such as drugs, medical devices, and aircraft. It also includes sector-specific requirements (for example, automotive, aerospace, telecommunications) and customer-imposed quality requirements.

- Training specifically targeted at the kind of internal auditing to be performed in the organization, including actual audit practice.

- Training on organization-specific requirements, including the scope and contents of the quality management system.

- Observing audits performed by others in the organization.

- Auditing under the supervision of a qualified auditor, either the audit boss or another individual who is authorized to make the decision that the candidate is capable of conducting internal audits.

At the risk of being repetitive, training is certainly desirable, especially for new or part-time auditors, but the focus must be on competence. A financial auditor in an organization, for example, may require a minimal amount of training in quality auditing to become competent, while an executive from marketing may require considerably more training (and practice under the supervision of a lead auditor) to become competent.

The audit boss also needs to consider providing annual refresher training to maintain the competence of the audit staff, both auditors and leaders. Topics for consideration in periodic refresher training include:

- Updates on standards

- Updates on changes to internal requirements

- Best practices from other organizations or from internal staff

- Highlights from the past year

- Case study exercises

- Effective report writing and interviewing

AUDITOR CERTIFICATION

A full-time or part-time audit staff may perform internal auditing. They all should be certified. One approach is to assign the audit boss the responsibility for certifying the team leaders (remember, a *team* may be only one auditor). The team leader could then be responsible for certifying the rest of the team members—for that audit only. They will be performing their duties only under the watchful eyes of the (already certified) team leader. Once a specific audit is completed and the audit boss accepts the report, those temporary certificates expire. Of course, if the audit boss has already qualified a team member, it is not necessary for that team member to be recertified by an audit team leader.

This approach ensures that the audit team leader is and remains competent and the members have received sufficient direction from the team leader. A variation of this approach is to only include organization-certified auditors in the audit pool. Then it is clear that management has designated the auditors as competent (and evidence would exist to support such a position).

Another approach is to use an individual who is experienced in conducting internal audits as a *master*. Apprentice auditors can learn from the master, who will then recommend certification to the audit boss when the apprentice is ready.

The function of audit teams and the roles of the team members will be described further in Part III, chapter 8, which is dedicated to audit planning.

Still another administrative responsibility for the audit boss is the management of a process for assessing auditor performance. Such a process could include the following:

- Review of the quality and timeliness of audit plans

- Review of the quality and timeliness of audit reports

- Active solicitation of customer feedback and perceptions

- Auditing the auditors

The audit boss should develop the criteria for certification of internal auditors (and associated records) to fit the needs of the organization. It is important, however, that at least *some* criteria be specified. The days of "just do it" should be long gone. It is not uncommon for an organization to require full-time audit team leaders to obtain ASQ Certified Quality Auditor (CQA) status. It is becoming increasingly popular to encourage individuals to achieve Registrar Accreditation Board (RAB) Certified Internal Auditor status. It is not typical or particularly valuable for individuals performing only internal audits to formally become RAB Certified Quality Management Systems Auditors, as that program is geared more toward professional third-party registration auditors.

Being the audit boss is an important and challenging assignment.

ETHICS—AGAIN

As a final note on auditors, it is worth repeating that internal auditors must adhere to a code of ethics, as was discussed in chapter 1. There are several professional codes of ethics relating to auditing. We recommend consideration of the one used for ASQ Certified Quality Auditors (see Figure 6.1). These ethical issues cover a few very simple but important concepts. Auditors need to be fair, objective, impartial, confidential, prudent, and honest.

To uphold and advance the honor and dignity of the profession, and in keeping with high standards of ethical conduct, I acknowledge that I:

Fundamental Principles

 I. Will be honest and impartial, and will serve with devotion my employer, my clients, and the public.

 II. Will strive to increase the competence and prestige of the profession.

 III. Will use my knowledge and skill for the advancement of human welfare, and in promoting the safety and reliability of products for public use.

 IV. Will earnestly endeavor to aid the work of the Society.

Relations with the Public

 1.1 Will do whatever I can to promote the reliability and safety of all products that come within my jurisdiction.

 1.2 Will endeavor to extend public knowledge of the work of the Society and its members that relates to public welfare.

 1.3 Will be dignified and modest in explaining my work and merit.

 1.4 Will preface any public statements that I may issue by clearly indicating on whose behalf they are made.

Figure 6.1   The ASQ code of ethics. Used by permission.   *Continued*

Continued

Relations with Employers and Clients

2.1 Will act in professional matters as a faithful agent or trustee for each employer or client.

2.2 Will inform each client or employer of any business connections, interests, or affiliations which might influence my judgment or impair the equitable character of my services.

2.3 Will indicate to my employer or client the adverse consequences to be expected if my professional judgment is overruled.

2.4 Will not disclose information concerning the business affairs or technical processes of any present or former employer or client without his consent.

2.5 Will not accept compensation from more than one party for the same service without the consent of all parties. If employed, I will engage in supplementary employment or consulting practice only with the consent of my employer.

Relations with Peers

3.1 Will take care that credit for the work of others is given to those to whom it is due.

3.2 Will endeavor to aid the professional development and advancement of those in my employ or under my supervision.

3.3 Will not compete unfairly with others; will extend my friendship and confidence to all associates and those with whom I have business relations.

Figure 6.1   The ASQ code of ethics. Used by permission.

7

Use of Audit Information and Results

Individual audit reports contain useful information. In addition to writing individual audit reports, there is a broader responsibility that should be considered—analyzing the patterns of all audits in the program. This aspect of audit program management is frequently ignored or informally performed. The audit boss, or others designated by management, should be systematically reviewing the audit reports collectively and looking for trends or opportunities for improvement that may not be obvious when noted in individual, stand-alone, unconnected audit reports. Suppose, for example, the audit boss has reviewed 10 audits conducted during the prior month and notices that there is a recurring problem with failure to analyze process or product data that has been gathered. For such a situation, the audit boss may recommend that a training module be developed and deployed on the effective use of analysis tools. Or perhaps the audit boss notices that there are several findings for instruments being out of service or having calibration schedules extended because of problems with an outside calibration lab. The audit boss could schedule a supplier audit of the lab to determine the cause of the problem and possible solutions. Or perhaps the audit boss does not see evidence that internal audits are concentrating on measuring process performance and analyzing results. This could point out a need for improvement in the organization's quality management system.

The audit boss should also look for a close coupling of nonconformities identified in the internal audit process with the corrective action process. In many organizations the audit boss is also responsible for maintaining the corrective action databases and for assuring that corrective action is implemented, that it is effective, and that it is institutionalized by documentation changes, training, and re-audit, as appropriate.

PERFORMING ANALYSES

Clause 8.4 of ISO 9001:2000 requires analysis of data to demonstrate the suitability and effectiveness of the quality management system. Even if this was not a requirement, it makes sense to squeeze as much information from audit results as possible. Since organizations may be performing several different kinds of audits, the data obtained may be quite diverse. The audit boss should consider the use of a variety of tools to analyze the data generated by internal audits. For example, use of graphs and charts, histograms, Pareto charts, cause-and-effect diagrams, and simple calculations of averages and dispersion (that is, variance) may be appropriate when attempting to extract information from a composite database of internal audit results.

 Let's consider possible areas that the audit boss could explore when reviewing data resulting from the internal audits.

Auditing for Compliance

- When we consolidate all deviations from requirements into one database, are there any trends?

- Are there any functions or processes that consistently have numerous audit issues?

- Are there generic training shortcomings (for example, with temporary workers)?

Auditing to Uncover Improvement Opportunities

- Are there best practices that could be applied elsewhere in the organization?

- Are all auditors seeking out opportunities for improvement?

- Are there any common threads in the opportunities uncovered?

- Are there any trends in process performance evident?

Auditing Individual Processes (For Example, a Production Work Cell)

- Is there evidence of consistent understanding of the link between functions, from business plans through achieving customer satisfaction?

- Are there any general issues with tools or infrastructure?

Auditing across Functional Lines

- Are there any common problems at process interfaces?

- Are there any systemic breakdowns common to several departments, for example, documentation?

- Are there any common communications issues?

- Are there any common personnel issues?

- Is there any evidence of consistent failure to meet requirements?

PRESENTING THE RESULTS OF THE ANALYSIS

The analysis of data from internal audits is an excellent source of information to be communicated throughout the organization, for discussion and consideration for action. Audit bosses are limited only by their own creativity in disseminating such information around the organization.

The management review process is an ideal forum in which the audit boss may present issues, areas of concern, and areas of opportunity for improvement of the quality management system that have surfaced through the analysis of internal audit data. There are several linked requirements embedded in ISO 9001:2000 that point to the use of management review to drive improvement in the organization. These requirements include clause 8.4 requiring analysis of data, clause 8.5.1 requiring continual improvement of the QMS through use of audit results as well as other actions, and clauses 5.6.1 and 5.6.2, which require top management to consider inputs from the results of audits to ensure continuing QMS suitability and to seek opportunities for improvement.

So the audit boss has an opportunity and an obligation to provide management and others in the organization, as appropriate, with a comprehensive assessment of issues related to the QMS. This should be done in as compelling a manner as possible. Some possibilities include:

- Creating an organizational intranet or LAN site for audit information. The audit boss could establish an informal communications mechanism for making information of general import widely available.

- Creating trend reports. Data can be presented in creative ways to highlight trends in improvement for products and functional areas, or for support organizations.

- Producing a periodic summary of all audit activity during a particular period of time.

Such a summary could take many different forms, from the very simple to the very complex, depending on the organization and the creativity of the audit boss. Table 7.1 illustrates an example.

Whatever approaches the audit boss uses to communicate information resulting from the audit program it is strongly recommended that issues be framed in monetary terms. For example, rather than stating "We have a continuing issue with defective final product A. This has been identified in each of the past three audits of this area." the audit boss could report "Defective product A, observed over the past nine months, has resulted in excess cost of $456,789 as measured by finance." The audit boss should always consider communicating in the language of business, which is cost, production, and risk.

When facts are presented to managers in a language that is readily understood (lost customers, wasted resources, rework, and expenditures),

Table 7.1 Audit analysis.

Audit Issue	Audit 1	Audit 2	Audit 3	Audit 4	. . .	Audit n	Total
Documentation							
Data analysis							
Competence							
Corrective action							
Control of nonconforming material							
. . .							

action to address a situation is more likely to occur. By being attentive to how internal audit information is communicated throughout the organization, the audit boss can profoundly influence the allocation of resources to improve performance in virtually every activity in the organization.

The audit boss can indeed be a powerful agent for positive change in the organization.

Part III

The Process of Auditing

INTRODUCTION

Parts I and II have discussed the basics of auditing and how to manage the audit program. Part III deals directly with the conduct of audits. It discusses the process of auditing from planning through the verification of corrective action. This part has four chapters.

Chapter 8 discusses the audit planning phase. It reviews the determination of audit objectives, the definition of the audit scope, determination of audit resources, preparation of the audit plan, document evaluation, and preparation of work papers.

Chapter 9 discusses the audit performance phase including both the process of auditing and personal aspects.

Chapter 10 provides a description of the audit reporting phase including the components of audit reports, how to write findings, how to write positive practices, the delivery of the oral report, and the delivery of the written report.

Chapter 11 covers the audit closure phase. It discusses options for closing out audits. It also discusses the documentation of issues to ensure that appropriate action is considered.

8

The Audit Planning Phase

FOUR PHASES OF THE AUDIT

An audit is a defined activity. It is a unique event that implements a portion of the overall audit program schedule (discussed earlier in part II, Audit Program Management). An audit may be considered to be a project, in that it has a beginning, a work phase, an output, and an end. There are four phases of the audit:

- Preparation

- Performance

- Reporting

- Closure

The preparation phase includes the activities necessary to get ready for data gathering. It starts with an assignment from the audit boss and ends when data collection commences. The preparation phase typically takes about 25 percent of the total time devoted to an individual audit.

The performance phase concerns itself with collection of data and analysis of those data. It starts with the on-site opening meeting and ends with the presentation of results at a closing meeting. There is some overlap between this phase and the following phase, reporting. The performance phase usually takes about half of the total audit time.

The reporting phase consists of the activity of presenting information to others outside of the audit team. It includes the informal closing meeting and the more formal written report. This phase is about 20 percent of the audit.

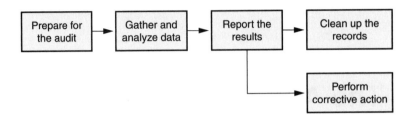

Figure 8.1 Audit processes.

Closure activities for just the audit are quite brief. After the report is prepared, delivered, and accepted by the audit boss, records are collected, assembled, and filed. Time sheets and expense reports, if applicable, must be completed. This takes very little time. If problems are uncovered, resulting corrective action on those problems will take considerable time. These closure activities are discussed in Chapter 11

Just as all quality management processes are linked into systems, these four phases may be also be seen as linked. The basic audit process is illustrated in Figure 8.1.

SEVEN ITEMS FOR AUDIT PLANNING

There are seven things that must be done before the data collection part of the audit starts. The audit boss will do some. The audit team members will do some:

1. Define the audit objectives.

2. Define the audit scope.

3. Define the audit resources.

4. Define the audit criteria.

5. Prepare and distribute the audit plan.

6. Understand and evaluate the written documents.

7. Prepare the work papers.

Each of these steps is also a process. The output of one step becomes the input for one or more subsequent steps.

DEFINE THE AUDIT OBJECTIVES

Before much else is attempted, the objectives of the audit must be defined. What is the reason for this particular audit? Why are resources being spent? How will it benefit the various stakeholders? These are all valid questions that should be discussed with the audit boss.

Auditing for Performance or Conformance?

As presented in chapter 4 of the first part of this book, audits are performed for two basic reasons: to determine if requirements are being met or to determine if there are opportunities for improvement. Both types of audits are necessary in today's environment. Certainly, highly regulated firms such as those producing medical devices will tend to audit more for compliance to rules and regulations. However, even the local Quick Copy shop has a need to assess compliance to internal and external rules.

On the other hand, competitors are challenging the way the organization operates. Government agencies are subjected to greater scrutiny with lower funding. Shareholders are demanding real improvements in operations. All of these pressures point to a need to use audits for improving the operations of the enterprise.

 Most of this discussion about audit purpose and objectives will take place when the audit boss canvasses the managers of the organization about the overall audit schedule. Now it is necessary to transmit those discussions to the individual auditors assigned to perform the audit. The audit team leader should meet with the audit boss and get a clear picture of the objectives. The team leader should then pass that information on to the team members. As mentioned in part I, the audit techniques, report contents, and expected follow-up actions will change depending on these objectives.

Who Are the Stakeholders (Customers)?

Every audit has customers. The actions taken to gather data, analyze facts, and report conclusions all have an effect on different parties. It is good to define these interested parties. What are the needs and desires (motivators)?

Of course, a major stakeholder of the audit is the auditee—the group being audited. Everyone wants to look good. The auditees want to be seen as competent and capable. As they become less fearful of the audit program, they will also begin to realize the consulting value of the audit. Having an outsider examine the operations from a fresh perspective might just be seen as free (and valuable) advice.

Another major stakeholder in the audit is the audit boss, who is the champion of the audit program to the other senior managers in the organization. The audit boss has made promises and now it is time to fulfill those promises. If any part of the audit process (preparation, performance, reporting, or closure) looks bad, the audit boss looks bad. He or she is accountable for the quality of the audit effort.

Finally, the audit should benefit the organization. It should add value to the operations of the organization by uncovering mistakes and oversights, by identifying systemic breakdowns, and by showing where greater efficiencies are possible. The audit about to be performed should contribute to the success of the enterprise. This is true for government as well as industry.

Interface with the Audit Boss

In defining the audit objectives, communication between the audit team leader and the audit boss needs to be strong. Together, they will define the purpose statement. Each audit should have its own unique purpose statement.

Typical Purpose Statements

Here are some typical statements for internal audits:

Purpose	Statement
Establish a baseline	The purpose of this audit is to verify that operational controls have been defined in the production area and are being implemented.
Monitor regulatory compliance	The purpose of this audit is to verify that current Good Laboratory Practices (cGLPs) are being implemented in the product-testing department.
Assess the effectiveness of final test	The purpose of this audit is to assess the effectiveness of final product test in assuring conformance to specified requirements
Assess packaging integrity	The purpose of this audit is to ensure specified processes are being followed in the packaging of products

DEFINE THE AUDIT SCOPE

The next step in preparation is to define the scope or boundaries of the audit. Once the boundaries are defined and made known to others, the audit should stay within these boundaries.

Determining the Processes to Be Audited

Recall that one of the most profound changes in the ISO 9000:2000 series of standards is the concept that organizations conduct their affairs by implementing a series of linked processes. As auditors, we must both understand and then measure those processes. (See discussion on the process approach in part I, chapter 2.) Since there are too many possible processes to examine, boundaries must be set. These boundaries are called the *scope* of the audit. They serve a practical need by limiting the investigation to something that can be accomplished within the allotted period of time. Boundaries also help the stakeholders to focus on specific areas in need of attention.

Determine the Functions of the Organization to Be Included

According to the *Quality Audit Handbook*, a *horizontal audit* is an audit of one system across several functional groups within the enterprise.[1] For example, part 6.2 of ISO 9001:2000 requires people performing work affecting product quality to be competent. It has five associated process activities:

1. Determine the competencies needed.

2. Provide training or other actions to fill the needed competencies.

3. Evaluate the effectiveness of training and other actions.

4. Ensure that people know how their jobs affect product quality.

5. Keep records of personnel education, training, skills, and experiences.

These five activities would likely be common among most of the functional groups in the firm, so it would be appropriate to do a horizontal audit to see how that common approach is working. The scope here would be the quality management system requirements for human resource controls (clause 6.2) within all departments of the company.

A *vertical audit* looks at many controls applied within a single functional group. The dispatch center of a transit company receives requests from riders and drivers and allocates resources to meet those needs. Within that dispatch center, processes must provide several things for success, including:

1. Competencies for using telephones and computers

2. Current information on routes and schedules

3. Current information on bus and driver availability

4. Rules and requirements for driving times and work breaks

All of these processes and activities have requirements that could be audited. The scope here could be the application of the quality management system within the bus dispatch center. Maintenance and advertising would then be considered to be outside of the scope.

As we discussed in part I, many audits will actually be a hybrid of these classic (horizontal and vertical) approaches. While we might focus on the human resources department (vertical audit), we also want to see how those controls are being applied throughout the enterprise (horizontal audit). We especially want to know if the processes are visible and being coordinated by senior management throughout the firm.

The audit boss should consider issues of horizontal and vertical when developing the audit schedule. Part II contains more details, but it is useful to review the thinking again during this audit-planning step.

What Is the Emphasis for the Audit?

One factor that influences the scope definition is the focus or emphasis. For example, suppose operational data are pointing to a possible problem in software configuration controls. The other aspects of the software lifecycle—high-level design requirements, module testing, and defect reporting—seem to be in pretty good shape. For this audit, management wishes to focus on configuration processes. The other areas might be excluded from the audit, so that sufficient time and effort may be devoted to software configuration issues.

Various Factors Affecting the Scope

The maturity of management processes will affect the scope. Early in the development of a quality management system, only the basics will be examined. The processes have not had time to stabilize and people are still somewhat unfamiliar with the concepts and their applications. As the quality management system matures, it becomes necessary to dig deeper. In a mature system, some of the well-established practices might be excluded from audits for a while. After all, how many times is it necessary to look at the same calibration stickers?

Maturity of the product production or service provision processes is another factor in determining the scope. When a production line first starts up, many things need to all work together. There are bound to be problem areas. These will be discovered and corrected. After a few years, the line runs quite smoothly (until equipment wear and tear begins to take hold). Early on, an audit in the area will focus on problem detection and correction. Later, the emphasis could shift to maintenance and performance improvement.

The history of previous audits in the area is a consideration. Areas found to be compliant earlier probably do not need as much attention later on. If previous audits show a pattern of difficulties in a particular area, the focus of the current audit should shift to that problem area. Along with previous audits, other continual improvement data (such as management reviews and corrective action reports) are used to determine the audit scope.

Interdepartmental relationships are often an impediment to quality. It can be quite difficult to overcome communication barriers and differing perspectives. Often, an audit that focuses on the inputs and outputs across departmental lines will uncover areas in need of management attention.

Time and activity within the audited group is a consideration. We must realize that the audit will always disrupt normal operations. There are certain periods when all the efforts of the group must be directed toward accomplishing the mission. Outsiders can be a dangerous distraction. If equipment used to manufacture rubber linings is down for a two-week period, for example, it would not be wise to audit the area.

Typical Scope Statements

Audit scope statements are generally *inclusive* rather than *exclusive*. This means they state the things to be audited, rather than stating the things to be avoided. Here are some examples:

- The scope of this audit includes planning and provisioning activities within the maintenance group.

- The scope of this audit will be training activities throughout the firm.

- The scope of the audit will be development of new software products, from determination of market and customer requirements through post-release customer feedback, and including design changes reacting to that feedback.

- The scope of this audit covers receiving inspection for the fairing assemblies.

- The scope of the audit will include determination of market needs, detailed customer requirements, and validation that our product designs meet those defined customer needs.

- The scope of this audit will focus on preventive maintenance activities within the past year in the operations and warehousing departments.

- The scope of the audit will be all production and support activities performed in the metal parts fabrication division.

- The scope of the audit will include the control and calibration of measuring devices within the research and development, design, engineering, testing, and production functions.

- The scope of the audit will be the service delivery process of bank tellers.

DEFINE THE AUDIT TEAM

The Audit Team

An audit team is one or more qualified auditors. The topic of auditor competencies and qualification is covered in depth in part II of this book. It is up to the audit team leader to work with the audit boss to assemble a qualified team for an audit.

Responsibilities

Audit team leaders are responsible for:

- Planning, organizing, and directing the audit

- Representing the team to the auditee and the audit boss

- Leading the team in reaching conclusions

- Preventing and resolving conflicts

- Preparing and completing the audit report

The team members are responsible for:

- Preparing for their assignments

- Gathering data and forming conclusions

- Contributing to the audit report

Subject matter experts are responsible for:

- Advising the team on possible sources of data

- Gathering data within their specialty area

- Assisting in the analysis of data within their specialty area

- Contributing to the technical accuracy of the report

Technical and Management Systems Knowledge

The audit team should have a balance of technical and management systems knowledge. They must understand the processes used to produce the goods and services. They must also understand the business processes used to manage the organization so as to achieve quality objectives. They must know the interrelationships of the functional departments within the enterprise. This combination is best obtained by using people who have broad experience in both the technical and administrative processes of the organization.

DEFINE THE AUDIT CRITERIA

As stated earlier, an audit is defined as a "systematic, independent and documented process for obtaining audit evidence and evaluating it objectively to determine the extent to which audit criteria are fulfilled."[2] This means that auditors must have some set of requirements (criteria) to which the gathered evidence can be compared. These *audit criteria* are defined as the "set of policies, procedures or requirements used as a reference."[3]

These audit criteria are also called the *basis* for the audit and are often depicted as a pyramid, as shown in Figure 8.2.

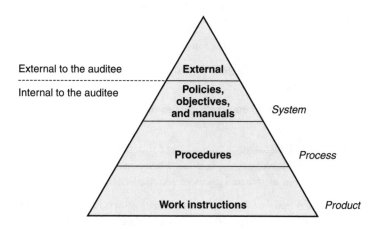

Figure 8.2 Basis for the audit.

Basic Rule of Auditing

 Without requirements (criteria) to match against the evidence, there can be no audit. Usually, the higher in the document pyramid, the more abstract the documents. As one gets closer to the work, the requirements become more specific.

External Requirements

External requirements originate from outside the location or site being audited. They can come from national and international sources. They can also come from government regulations. External requirements may also come from corporate headquarters, so they apply to all units of the firm. Of course, they also come from the external customer. Here are some examples of external requirements:

- International trade agreements, such as the World Trade Organization

- International consensus standards, such as the ISO 9001:2000 document

- National regulations, such as the U.S. Code of Federal Regulations (CFR)

- National consensus standards, such as the ANSI Z1.11 standard for training and education

- Industry codes and standards, such as those promulgated by the American Association of Blood Banks or the Institute of Food Technology

- Package labels and inserts found on regulated products and devices

- Corporate policy, designed to provide consistent direction across the enterprise

- Customer requirements, reflected in the contract and purchasing specifications

- Market and customer requirements for better products, improved services, or lower prices, that have been accepted by senior management as internal goals or requirements

With the exception of package labels and inserts, external documents generally give broad requirements but do not give direction on how to accomplish these requirements. (One could argue that many industry specifications, package labels, and customer requirements are quite detailed and certainly not generic. Customer pressures for better quality or lower prices may be viewed as abstractions until they are translated into internal requirements. While true, it is still convenient to put all of these external documents into one category.)

Internal Requirements

Internal documents tell how to apply the external requirements to specific processes, sites, and functions. They describe internal management systems for areas of the organization such as quality, environment, research, or finance.

At the highest (internal) level are those transition documents giving the framework for the local operations. These are often called policies, objectives, and manuals. Top management should have a set quality policy and quality objectives. The quality management system should have been established in such a way that it is focused on meeting those objectives and enhancing customer satisfaction. There may be a single manual for the whole organization. Alternatively, there may be several of these manuals, one for each section, department, or division. They describe how the external requirements will be implemented at a particular site, facility, or location. The manual(s) describe how processes interact—how they work together to meet the organization's quality objectives.

Procedures describe processes. They give the step-by-step requirements for the activity. Procedures provide generic process instructions. They usually provide direction on how to implement external requirements and meet internal quality objectives at the operational level, so one would expect to see manufacturer's instructions and regulatory requirements reflected in a procedure. Depending on the firm and the goods and services being produced, there may be quite a number of different procedures. Examples include:

- Standard operating procedures

- Quality system procedures

- Training procedures

- Calibration procedures

- Start-up and shutdown procedures

- Maintenance procedures

- Emergency procedures

- Design procedures

- Records procedures

- Customer complaint procedures

- Loan application procedures

Figure 8.3 illustrates requirements for an audit of a cell growth process.

There are times when it becomes necessary to provide criteria for a specific task. Work instructions are task- or component-specific. A recipe for making peanut butter cookies would be a work instruction. Other examples include weld diagrams, inspection plans, and postal codes to use during a telemarketing campaign. Such instructions provide the details important to obtaining an output from a given process that meets requirements.

These external and internal documents are not the only sources of information for the audit. They are the *basis* or *criteria* for the audit about

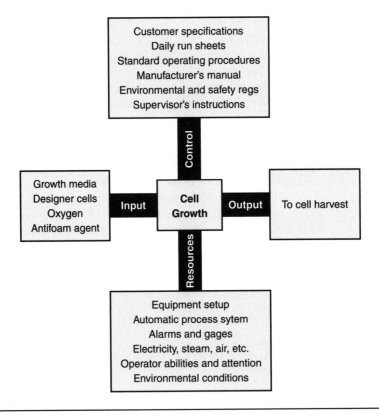

Figure 8.3 Requirements for the audit.

to be performed. Other documents, such as process flow diagrams, job descriptions, and design review notes, will be used in preparing for the audit. These other documents will allow the auditors to better understand the environment about to be examined.

Obtaining the Documents

With assistance from the audit boss, the team should define and then review the documents about to be used as the basis for the upcoming audit. It is not absolutely necessary to obtain the latest (controlled) versions, as that control will probably be examined during the next (performance) phase. However, the documents examined should be reasonably recent, to avoid developing data collection plans and checklists that are based on documents that are not representative of the process to be audited.

Several sources are available for obtaining the documents:

- Central technical library of command media
- Department document clerks or coordinators
- Departmental quality engineers and specialists
- Documents in the audit files (if still current and applicable)
- Online, from the document file server or intranet

Perhaps the best way to discover which documents apply within the defined audit scope is to ask the auditee. Of course, this should be an informal contact, in person, by telephone, or by e-mail.

Output Is a List

Once the criteria for the audit are defined, they should be captured in writing. The common way to accomplish this is by making a list. The list should include external as well as internal documents. Reviewing the list of documents with the audit boss once or twice is a good idea.

PREPARE THE AUDIT PLAN

By now, there should be sufficient information to develop an *audit plan*. The audit plan is a handy place to keep all the information associated with the upcoming audit. It is unique to each audit.

The *audit plan* is not the same as the *audit schedule*. The audit boss produces the audit schedule, after consultation with other managers in the firm. It shows the audits planned for a period of time (generally a year), when they are scheduled, and perhaps even who will be the team leader. Each specific audit has a separate audit plan.

Contents of the Audit Plan

 The audit team leader, in consultation with the rest of the audit team, develops the audit plan. It contains the following items:

- Purpose or objectives of the audit

- Scope and boundaries of the audit

- Identification of audit team members

- Criteria for the audit

- Anticipated start and stop dates and times

- Audit interfaces, if any

After the audit team has defined these items, it is a good idea (and may be a requirement) to have the plan approved by the audit boss. This improves the communication between the audit team and the audit boss. It also contributes to the checks and balances associated with auditing.

Formal Notification

In the spirit of cooperation and full exchange of information, it is a good idea (though not required) to send the audit plan to the auditee. This is done through the audit boss, after the plan is approved. Recommended practice is to send the audit plan as an e-mail attachment, from the audit boss to the manager of the audited area. Many internal audit organizations are finding that such notification 30 days before the opening meeting is desirable. Not only does this discourage last-minute procrastination, but it also encourages the free exchange of information between the two parties.

REVIEW, STUDY, AND UNDERSTAND THE DOCUMENTS

The audit team members should study the documents to understand the systems and their processes. Often, the team leader will divide the scope into smaller portions. Each team member can then study and review their assigned area. Periodically during the planning stage, the team should get together to compare notes and assess their progress.

First, the team should understand the organization's quality policy and associated quality objectives. Since these objectives must be measurable, it is useful for the team to review the data on progress toward meeting them. As the actual audit progresses, the team should look for alignment of process measures and targets with these overall quality objectives.

The second part of the review is to truly understand the production and service delivery processes as well as the processes for management and support. These are described in local documents, that is the documents that relate to the area being audited. It is here that the process approach to auditing becomes most meaningful. (Refer back to part I, chapters 2 and 3, for a detailed discussion.) Each auditor must understand process inputs, outputs, controls, and resources. Auditors should also be familiar with technical conditions that lead to process success and failure.

Production and Service Delivery Processes

Clause 7.5 of ISO 9001:2000 covers control over production and service provision. These are the so-called *factory processes*, because they deal with making the items or delivering the services. They relate to the specific actions used to produce goods and services.

Management and Support Processes

The management and support processes support the factory processes. These are the things we do to understand customer requirements, provide for human and equipment capital, communicate within the organization, and the host of other things done to run the business or agency.

Flowcharting and Process Mapping

Many auditors find it useful to draw a flowchart of the operations about to be audited. What processes are performed and what are the linkages? This also helps to define the interfaces where information and other resources come into and flow out of the audited area. If process maps already exist (and it is highly likely with the process approach to quality management encouraged by ISO 9001:2000), they should be used to help the auditors understand the various process relationships.

Many auditors find this part of the preparation process quite demanding. This may be particularly true if the auditors do not have extensive knowledge of the work processes. Typically, auditors are not resident technical experts. On the other hand, they should know the details as well as the big picture. This requires preparation. Individual study of documents such as the following will help:

- Audit files of previous audits in the area

- Process descriptions and procedures

- Internet and intranet searches

Normally, individual study is not always sufficient. Additional sources of information could be:

- Colleagues who are familiar with the area and its processes

- Subject matter experts, if any are on the audit team

While it is certainly permissible (and often desirable) to ask someone from the audited area to explain the work flow and process steps, team members should be careful not to start auditing during this study phase.

Review the Documents for Adequacy

The work controls should flow down from policy to activity. Certain documents should be considered valid from the start: ISO 9001:2000 standard, government regulations, corporate policy, and customer requirements. These are all external requirements or high-level policy. Difficulty often comes in making the transition from policy to practice. Sometimes, the policy is not understood, so the implementation documents are vague or meaningless. Sometimes, the policy is misunderstood and implementation is incorrect. These lower-level documents should be reviewed to determine their conformity to higher requirements. Document review will provide input to developing the audit work papers.

What to Do When Documents Appear to Be Inadequate

If the document review shows that the written controls are missing or inadequate, the audit team member should first contact the auditee for clarification. Chances are, the information exists somewhere. There are also perfectly valid cases where a process may not require documentation. This is discussed further in part I, chapter 3. If subsequent investigation continues to show that the required written controls are unsatisfactory, there is a possibility the audit may have to be canceled or postponed. This is not a decision made lightly, or by the auditors. The audit boss makes this decision, but only after consulting with the audit team leader, managers of the affected areas, and other stakeholders.

Prepare Work Papers

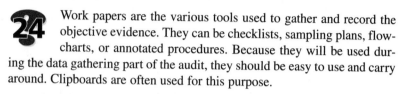 Work papers are the various tools used to gather and record the objective evidence. They can be checklists, sampling plans, flowcharts, or annotated procedures. Because they will be used during the data gathering part of the audit, they should be easy to use and carry around. Clipboards are often used for this purpose.

Develop Process Flow

To make maximum use of the process approach to auditing, the work papers should reflect the flow of activities to be audited. The process approach is discussed in detail in part I, chapter 2. Figure 8.4 shows a basic process. Using the flowcharts and process maps developed earlier, focus on the facts necessary to explore process inputs and outputs, as well as process controls and resources.

Rarely can a set of work papers be recycled for another audit without modification. Too many of the variables (purpose, scope, team composition, areas of interest, stakeholder needs, and so on) may have changed. Many find that a common set, customized for the current audit by adding, removing, and modifying questions, works best.

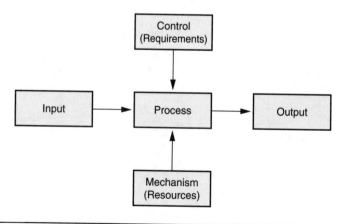

Figure 8.4   Generic process model.

Work papers will always undergo modification during the actual audit. Plan on it. Some areas will exhibit greater controls than originally expected and in-depth evaluation will no longer be necessary. Other areas will have significant problems and much more data will be needed for the investigation. Team members will find common issues midway through the audit and peripheral data will need to be gathered. All of this means that work papers should be designed from the beginning for change.

Examples of Various Approaches

 The two common layouts for the audit checklist are columnar form and free-form. The columnar form forces decision making on the spot by requiring a yes–no or satisfied–unsatisfied conclusion for each piece of information gathered. Figure 8.5 shows an example of the columnar form of audit checklist.

This approach can result in very precise information if each question focuses on a single piece of data. The visual display of yes or no tick marks helps to organize the data for analysis and developing findings and conclusions. It can also be abused if the questions become more judgmental. The neophyte auditor may tend to form conclusions based on insufficient factual information, causing later encounters during the closing meeting to become quite heated as memory fades.

 The free-form layout promotes greater flexibility. Its emphasis is on data, whether compliant or noncompliant. Figure 8.6 shows an example of the free-form layout of the audit checklist.

The free-form style promotes gathering of facts from many sources and levels. Unfortunately, the neophyte auditor is often left wondering, "How much is enough before I can move on to the next question?" Field notes tend to be messy and may have the appearance of disorganization.

Requirement	Yes	No	N/A	Notes
First question (reference)				
Second question (reference)				
Third question (reference)				

Figure 8.5 Columnar form of audit checklist.

Audit checklist 23-03

1. First question is written here, across the entire page, using word wrap. At the end of the question, the reference is shown in parentheses. The question is followed by blank space to allow for handwritten notes in the field.

2. The second question follows the first in a similar fashion.

3. The third question follows.

Figure 8.6 Example of free-form layout of audit checklist.

However, this can lead to greater exchange of ideas during team meetings and prior to the closing meeting. Both forms of the checklist have stood the test of time. Either is acceptable.

THE PREPARATION PACKAGE

The products (or outputs) of the preparation activities include:

• Clearly defined objectives, scope, and criteria for the audit

• Team identification and assignments

• Specific audit plan for the upcoming audit

• Flowcharts or maps of the processes, areas, and activities about to be examined

• Review and preliminary analysis of the formal (documented) requirements

• Communication and agreement with the parties about to be audited

• Work papers to define information needs

• An initial idea of the time and resources that will be necessary to perform the remainder of the audit

Total resources (people and time) devoted to preparation should usually be about half of the planned resources for the data-gathering part of the audit. This is time well spent.

ENDNOTES

1. ASQ Quality Audit Division, J. P. Russell, editing director, *The Quality Audit Handbook*, 2nd ed. (Milwaukee: ASQ Quality Press, 2000): 160.
2. ISO 9000:2000, 3.9.1
3. Ibid, 3.9.3

9

Audit Performance Phase

The preceding chapter described in detail the planning and preparation effort required prior to commencing an audit. If the planning and preparation are inadequate, then the audit will most likely be a waste of time for both the auditor and auditee. Auditors have an ethical responsibility to be prepared to perform a thorough and comprehensive audit that is respectful of the time of the auditee. When auditors follow the preparation steps described in the preceding chapter, they will be adequately prepared to actually conduct an internal audit.

PROCESS AND PERSONAL ASPECTS

Internal audits have two aspects: a process-related aspect and a personal aspect. The process aspect covers actions taken to conduct a meaningful audit. The personal aspect covers how to perform those actions.

There is no single right way to do an audit. Auditing is not like mathematics where there is only one right answer to the question "What is 1 + 1?" Auditing is about understanding requirements, looking for opportunities for improvement, looking for best practices, asking questions, gathering information, analyzing what is seen and heard, forming opinions, and reaching conclusions. Much of this effort requires that auditors exercise good judgment. It is not unheard of (but it is very unusual) for two competent auditors to audit the same activity and reach different conclusions. Indeed, if 10

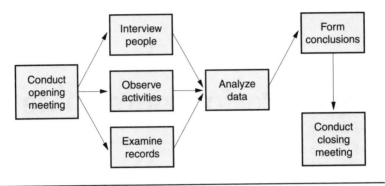

Figure 9.1 Performance phase of the audit.

competent auditors audited the same activity the result would (or should) be 10 similar but slightly different conclusions and 10 similar but slightly different audit reports depending on who the auditors talked with, how they sampled quality records, what documents were reviewed, what objective evidence was available at the time of the audit, the overall knowledge of the auditor about the processes audited, and how information is analyzed.

To minimize these differences, auditors should be prepared (which includes having the competence necessary to perform the audit), conscientious, fair, objective, and impartial. Keep in mind that auditing is an acquired skill, not a talent inherently embedded in an individual's DNA. It takes practice to be a good auditor and the best way to improve auditing skills is to perform audits, in the company of an experienced auditor if possible.

PROCESS ASPECTS OF THE PERFORMANCE PHASE

Now what are the process aspects of internal auditing? The process is shown in Figure 9.1. Here is a list of activities that should be considered for each audit:

- Holding an opening meeting with the manager of the area to be audited

- Observing processes

- Observing process outputs, including final product, if applicable

- Asking questions

- Gathering objective evidence of the extent to which requirements are being met or not met

- Keeping great notes

- Analyzing objective evidence

- Synthesizing all that is seen and heard and draw conclusions

- Holding a closing meeting with the manager of the audited area

KEEP AUDIT OBJECTIVES IN MIND

While performing these process duties, internal auditors need to keep the objectives of the audit in mind. Recall that these objectives were defined in the audit plan (see previous chapter). Are we to determine if requirements are being met or are we also looking for improvement opportunities? Both objectives require the auditor to be constantly alert for clues. This is not an easy task. It requires experience, process knowledge, ability to detect connections, and a very open mind. If the objective is to uncover and encourage transfer of best practices, then the auditor must be able to detect such practices. If an objective is to identify and recognize exceptional performance and attitudes by individuals, then the auditor must be able to distinguish between acceptable and great.

Auditors should review the objectives defined in the audit plan prior to starting an audit. We recommend audit objectives be a mix of seeking:

- The extent to which requirements are being met

- Opportunities for improvement

- Best practices that possibly can be transferred to other areas (cross-fertilization of practices between individuals or groups)

- Outstanding performance and attitudes

The auditor has a challenging task to keep all these objectives in mind during the course of the audit.

PERSONAL ASPECTS OF THE PERFORMANCE PHASE

Personal characteristics refer to the ways auditors conduct themselves when performing audits. These include:

- Interviewing skills

  - Listening skills

- What to do when no documented procedures are available

- Asking questions

- Summarizing

- Observing

- Being respectful of auditees

• Time management

• Handling uncertainty, ambiguity, and conflict

• Personal hygiene

When performing an audit, many of the process and personal characteristics identified occur simultaneously. For example, while observing processes, auditors may be asking questions, gathering evidence, listening, forming opinions, and reaching conclusions. These items are being identified and discussed individually to ensure an understanding of each, but an experienced auditor will be able to perform these different activities simultaneously while working toward the successful completion of the audit assignment.

OPENING MEETING

Before actually gathering data, the audit team (remember, a team can be an individual) should meet with the manager or supervisor of the area or function being audited. The format for an opening meeting is flexible. It can be held in the office of the manager representing the activity being audited, on the manufacturing floor, or in a conference room. It may be a sit-down meeting or a quick stand-up meeting. The opening meeting is an opportunity for the auditors to introduce themselves and to describe the audit plan and process. It is important to make sure that audit objectives are clear, answer any questions, and put the auditee at ease. The auditors should also indicate the time expected to complete the interviews, observe activities, record reviews, and address any other items included in the audit plan. The team leader should stress that the intent of internal audits is to focus on process, not to find fault with people. In other words, auditors should strive to create a non-adversarial environment for the audit. If daily briefings are desired (and they normally are for audits lasting more than a day), the time and place should be defined. Finally, arrangements for a closing meeting should be made.

The extent of the opening meeting is typically related to the scope and objectives of the audit. Audits with broad scopes and objectives require a more formal and extensive opening meeting.

Things that should be done in every opening meeting include:

- Introducing all parties

- Reviewing the audit objectives and scope

- Determining the general flow and assignments for data gathering (who will be with whom and when)

- Making arrangements for a closing meeting

- Reviewing safety concerns

- Reviewing housekeeping and communications (escorts, briefings, and so on)

Every audit, no matter how large or small, should have an opening meeting. It can be as short as two minutes or as long as an hour. To avoid wasting valuable audit time, the team leader should take charge, maintain control, and keep it moving.

OBSERVE THE PROCESSES

The auditor must observe the processes of the area being audited. If a flowchart or process map has been constructed in planning the audit (or already existed as an element of process documentation) this can be used to guide the auditor. Here the auditor probes to assess the degree to which the processes are operating in conformity to requirements. If improvement is an audit objective, the auditor needs to be alert for areas that could be considered for improvement, as well as any other audit objective contained in the audit plan.

Here are some things to consider when observing any process:

- What are the objectives of the work center, area, process, activity, or product being observed?

- How do these relate to the overall objectives of the organization? To the quality policy? Are they consistent? Is there alignment?

- Does everyone involved know what the customer requirements are (both internal and external)?

- Is there an understanding of what is necessary to meet (or exceed) those customer requirements?

- Are individuals performing the work correctly? Do they know what to do and have the means to do it, including documentation, time, and tools?

- Are the requirements for successful completion of work clear?

- How do individuals know that they have performed the work to requirements? Are process or product metrics in place and being used?

- What is done with data that are collected related to the product or process? Who analyzes it? For what purpose? Is there evidence of use of the analyzed data?

- How is continual improvement addressed for the activity being observed?

- What happens when deviations from requirements are found? What are the processes for:

  - Correction

  - Control of nonconforming product

  - Disposition of nonconforming product

  - Analysis for possible corrective action

  - Use of the data for preventive action, when applicable

- Is there evidence of any best practices or approaches that can be applied elsewhere in the organization?

- Do the inputs to the process being observed meet specified requirements?

- Are requirements defined for the processes being observed and understood by internal suppliers?

- How is internal supplier performance measured? Is there a feedback mechanism to those suppliers?

- How is customer feedback (external or internal) solicited and used for the processes being observed?

The auditor needs to keep in mind that every process in the organization should be functioning to achieve internal and external customer satisfaction.

Processes should be aligned with (or at least not be in conflict with) other processes of the organization, with business objectives, and with the quality policy and objectives. The work of an internal auditor is indeed challenging!

OBSERVE ACTIVITY RESULT

In addition to observing the processes of the area being audited, the auditor should observe products and outputs. The generic questions above will help. Are customer requirements (external or internal) for the product known and understood? Are they being met? How do we know? Is objective evidence available?

NO DOCUMENTED PROCEDURES AVAILABLE

The new ISO 9001:2000 has considerably de-emphasized the role of documentation in the overall structure of the QMS of an organization. Now, documented procedures are specifically required in only six areas:

1. Control of documents

2. Control of records

3. Control of nonconforming product

4. Internal audit

5. Corrective action

6. Preventive action

But auditors still need to see if processes are being planned and carried out under controlled conditions. So, what is an auditor to do when no documented procedures exist? These actions may help an auditor to determine if processes are functioning according to requirements:

- Ask several workers. Are the answers consistent?

- Ask supervisors. Is there a credible message as to how the workers know what to do, and is there consistency between the supervisor's view and the workers' actions?

- Look for competent work. Is there evidence that process output meets requirements?

- Look at process and product metrics. Are they consistent with expectations?

- Look for alignment of the work being performed with objectives, quality policy, and organizational strategy, as appropriate.

Lack of documented procedures is not, in itself, evidence of lack of control. The auditor needs to understand the process and judge its adequacy to produce output consistent with requirements.

PAUSE FOR REFLECTION

For audits of more than a few hours, it is often necessary to take one or more breaks while observing activities and products. The team needs to assess the progress of the audit versus the plan. They also need to address any issues that arise during the course of audit. These breaks should be conducted in a quiet place and away from the auditees. Twice a day is common for audits lasting longer than one day. Three areas need to be explored in team (caucus) meetings:

- Where are you in the audit plan?

- What are the issues that seem to be forming?

- What additional data is needed and do you have time left to collect it?

ASK QUESTIONS

 The primary way auditors obtain information is by asking questions. Therefore, auditors need to practice the art of asking questions.

There are two basic kinds of questions auditors can ask—open-ended questions and closed questions. An open-ended question is intended to encourage a response from an auditee. Open-ended questions usually start with:

- Who?

- What?

- When?

- Where?

- Why?

- How?

- Please show me . . .

A closed question would be, "Is today Tuesday?" It is used to get a brief and succinct answer. Generally, auditors should try to ask open-ended questions, since the answers to such questions are rich in information about process performance and personnel competence.

The preferred style of asking questions is not that of a federal prosecutor, but more in the manner of Gandhi. A soft-spoken approach will maximize the opportunity to elicit the desired information from the auditee. One very effective way of doing this is to treat the discussion as a conversation about the work being performed. Asking closed questions (questions that can be answered yes or no) usually does not work.

In conducting the interview, auditors must get close to the activities (processes) being performed. It is much better for auditors to go to the workers than to have the workers come to the auditors. Auditors must know about the processes and tap the wisdom of those performing the processes. Process-based auditing requires this approach.

GATHER OBJECTIVE EVIDENCE

Auditors should seek objective evidence to corroborate verbal assertions of compliance with requirements. Not because an auditor suspects that an auditee is lying, rather because the communication between the two parties is often less than optimal. The auditee may not hear or understand the questions and the auditor may not hear or understand the answers. If, for example, the supervisor says there is a daily requirement to measure the sugar content of a vat of fermenting wine, the auditor can, and should, request to see the record of that measurement. If a welfare office has a requirement to log the arrival time of each applicant, the auditor should review the actual log sheet.

In many cases, it is best for the auditor to record important data from the examined material in their field notes, rather than request copies. This makes the audit go faster (more efficient) and minimizes the hassle factor for the auditee. It also shows a degree of trust toward fellow employees. When the environment is adversarial or the risk of regulatory action is great, copies may be appropriate. These notes and copies become the raw data for reaching conclusions and preparing an audit report, which is covered in the next chapter.

KEEP GREAT NOTES

Unless an auditor has a photographic memory, it is essential to take notes during the course of an audit. It is better to have too many notes than too few. Good notes will minimize the struggles to remember the contents of a design review package examined, or the evidence of the completion of a required test.

Of course, the auditor needs to keep the audit plan in mind, watch the time, and ask pertinent questions. Auditors must listen to and hear answers. They must take great notes!

ANALYZE INFORMATION

In performing the audit, an auditor sees, hears, and obtains records. What is one to do with all this input? It is the responsibility of an auditor to *think*. "What are the data telling me about the process or function?" In other words, auditors need to analyze the facts they obtain. It may not be enough for an auditor to just look at an X-bar and R control chart being maintained for a shaft diameter. They need to ask themself, "Does the chart demonstrate a process operating under controlled conditions? Does the operator understand the chart? Should we consider a c-chart? Is there an opportunity for improving the process?"

SYNTHESIS OF ALL THAT IS SEEN AND HEARD AND REACHING CONCLUSIONS

After an auditor has completed the quest for understanding the performance of a function or process there is a need to put it all together. The audit team has an obligation to reach conclusions and form an opinion of whether the processes and resulting systems are operating under controlled conditions. In fact, one could argue that ensuring that processes are operating under controlled conditions is the essence of quality management. With control comes quality.

Typically auditors should reach conclusion in the following areas:

- Is there evidence of failure to meet requirements?

  - If so, is the failure an isolated event or is it systemic?

  - What are the threads and connections to other processes and applications?

- Are there any areas that should be noted for consideration of action to improve performance, such as lowering cost, reducing rework, improving output, or increasing throughput?

- Are there any best practices that can be suggested for consideration by other areas of the enterprise?

- Are there any individuals or group who displayed uncommon diligence, professionalism, or attitude that merits special recognition?

HOLD A CLOSING MEETING

 The auditor should always hold a closing meeting, if only to tell the auditee that they are leaving. Of course, closing meetings should be much more meaningful. These meetings should include at least the following:

- A brief summary of what was examined and why (scope and objectives)

- An overall opinion on the application of the quality management system within the areas just examined

- Any positive practices observed

- Any occurrences of failure to comply with requirements, and whether such occurrences were isolated or systemic

- As necessary, sharing with the auditee the objective evidence to substantiate any occurrences of failure to comply with requirements

- Any unusual events or practices or anything unexpected that was observed

- Resolution of any areas of disagreement over objective evidence or auditor conclusions

- Explaining the process for corrective action on any significant adverse findings

It is worth repeating that an auditor should never surprise an auditee by including anything negative in an audit report that has not been discussed with the auditee. This is one of the fastest and surest ways of destroying the effectiveness of the internal audit program.

PERSONAL CHARACTERISTICS

Auditors also possess personal characteristics that influence their auditing. Some of these characteristics are a function of the inherent personality of the auditor, but others can be learned and improved with practice. Let's consider a few of these characteristics.

Listening Skills

Auditors must ask questions. There is an old Italian proverb that says, "When you ask a question, be prepared to listen to and accept the answer." If the auditor asks, "Would you tell me how you do your job?" he or she needs to actively listen to the answer and determine what is *meant* by the answer. Sometimes that which is *not* said is more important than that which is said. If the auditee offers imprecise or evasive answers, for example, the auditor can ask follow-up questions until the auditor hears the answer to the question (or determines that an answer will not be forthcoming). Auditors can also listen for trigger words, such as "We always do this" or "We never do that," and be prepared to authenticate the validity of the auditee's statement or to probe more deeply.

Observational Skills

While interviewing and asking questions and actively listening, auditors need to maintain a wide field of vision—observing everything occurring in the area being audited. Subtle clues typically abound that indicate the real situation. These clues may even contradict what the auditee says. For example, an auditee may say "We always put the subassembly on the pallet after test." At the same time a coworker places a subassembly on a rack next to untested subassembles. Or, "We always stamp the PC board immediately after completing that test," is uttered while the auditor observes a coworker stamping an entire box of PC boards.

Observing body language can provide clues about the true situation. The classic folded arms demeanor of an auditee is said to indicate a reluctance to be open with the auditor. Or it may just mean she's cold! Body language can help to provide insight into the true situation. Auditors should be aware of body language and use common sense and caution in interpreting it.

Auditors also need to be attentive to their own body language, keeping in mind their professional responsibility to be impartial and objective. Auditors should avoid actions such as rolling of eyes or exhibiting aggressive behavior toward auditees.

Asking Questions

Auditors ask questions. How they ask the questions can make a difference in the quality and quantity of the answers they receive. Asking questions was discussed earlier in the section on process characteristics of audits, but it is worth repeating on the personal side. Carefully consider the kinds of questions asked of the auditee. Open-ended questions are used to gain broad insight. Closed questions are appropriate to obtain very specific pieces of information. Closed questions can also be used to redirect an auditee who is too verbose.

Auditors should feel no inhibition when asking for objective evidence. The more evidence the auditor can see during the course of the audit, the better the final report. That report will also be easier to write.

Summarizing

Auditors must stay on their plan, and time is frequently a constraint. One graceful way of closing a conversation with an auditee is to summarize the discussion. This will demonstrate that the auditor understands the situation and help to terminate the discussion. This paraphrasing and summarizing technique should be used frequently during the audit. It shows that the auditor has been listening to the auditee and it enables the auditor to move on to other aspects of the audit plan.

Having Respect for the Auditee

Auditors must exude a profound respect for auditees. Auditees must be treated with respect and consideration. Special care may be required with frontline workers, who may not be experienced with interaction with auditors. They might view such encounters as quite stressful. In some audit environments, a union representative must be present during interviews to act as a buffer for this stress. Auditors should do their best to put their fellow associates at ease. It often helps to state that the audit focus is on process and not about finding fault with people. A variant of the golden rule should govern—"Treat others during an audit as you would like to be treated."

Time Management

Time can be an ally or enemy of the auditor. Typically, time will pressure an auditor. There always seems to be more to see, more to look at, more questions to ask, and more evidence to gather than there is time to do all these things.

This is why thorough planning is an essential step in conducting an internal audit, and why time must be carefully managed during the course of an audit. Auditors need to pay attention to their plan and to the schedule. If examination of a process area is scheduled for four hours and the plan includes 18 items to consider, it does not take a mathematician to determine that at the two-hour point the auditor should be more than halfway through the items to be addressed. (Don't forget time for the closing meeting!) It definitely helps to wear a watch.

It is common sense and respectful of the auditee to adhere to the committed schedule. If unforeseen events occur, or if major issues are uncovered, it may be necessary and appropriate to suspend the audit or to schedule additional time to complete it. Such action should be by mutual agreement between the auditor, the audit boss, and the manager of the area being audited.

Handling Uncertainty, Ambiguity, and Conflict

The world of auditing includes elements of uncertainty and ambiguity. This should not be a source of concern—that's the real world. Auditors need to address uncertainty and ambiguity by gathering as much pertinent information as possible, analyzing the information, and reaching conclusions. If a circumstance of importance is not clear or if an auditor cannot determine if a requirement is consistently being fulfilled or that a process is operating under controlled conditions, then the facts, including the uncertainty or ambiguity, can be discussed in the closing meeting and described in the audit report.

Regarding conflict, it is unprofessional for an auditor to be in a conflict situation with an auditee. Also, it is inappropriate for an auditor to argue with the auditee.

Personal Hygiene, Appearance, and Actions

A somewhat sensitive subject but an important one, is the need for auditors to be attentive to personal hygiene and appearance. Effective use of dental floss, mouthwash, breath mints, and deodorant should be sufficient to ensure that auditors do not create an unpleasant or uncomfortable environment when conducting an audit. Auditors should also dress in a professional manner appropriate to the process area requirements. Solid shoes, lab coats, and the like may be required for all in the area being audited. Auditors must always follow the rules, even if others disobey them, and should be particularly attentive to safety rules.

CAUTION AREAS

When conducting audits, there are situations where auditors need to be extra attentive. Following are a few of the most common caution areas to consider.

Things Auditors Do to Auditees

• *Being too soft on the auditee.* For example, "Because you are my mother I am not going to document the fact that you failed to follow the work instruction requiring the use of a wrist strap when handling a static-sensitive circuit board."

• *Being too hard on the auditee.* "I don't care that you are my brother, I still want you to produce the last four years of evidence that you tested every subassembly shipped."

• *Not listening.* After asking a question, failing to actively listen to the auditee's answer; this behavior nonverbally communicates disrespect for the auditee.

• *Arguing with auditee.* As mentioned above, it is inappropriate and unprofessional for an auditor to argue with or criticize an auditee.

• *Providing advice while auditing.* As tempting as it may be, it is inappropriate for an auditor to act as an advisor or get involved in decisions related to what action to take while conducting an audit. It may be appropriate, after the audit is completed, for an auditor to respond to a request for input on an issue.

• *Exceeding the scope of an audit.* It is easy for auditor to go beyond the scope of the audit. This must be avoided. If there are issues that are appropriate to explore that are beyond the scope of the audit, note these in the closing meeting and in the audit report and suggest the possibility of an additional or follow-up audit.

• *Poor time management.* As was mentioned above, auditors need to pay attention to meeting commitments on audit timing and to complete the audit on schedule. It is an imposition on an auditee to exceed the time schedule for the audit, unless by mutual agreement.

• *Reporting too many minor negative items.* An internal audit should ascertain that processes are being carried out in accordance with planned requirements and, if part of the objectives, look for opportunities for improvement. When deviations from requirements are noted, they should be reported in a way that expedites corrective action. It does not add value to report many trivial items, especially when such reporting obscures meaningful corrective action on important items.

Things Auditees Do to Auditors

• *Providing misleading answers or answers to different questions than the auditor asked.* Occasionally, auditees will intentionally or unintentionally answer a different question than the one the auditor asked, or provide a misleading or evasive answer. Auditors should politely re-ask the question. If this approach does not produce the desired result, the auditor can state "I am trying to get an answer to this question, but we do not seem to be communicating so I will note this as an issue." Alternatively, an auditor could ask "With whom can I speak to get more details?" or "Who else may have some information about this?" Adopting a conversational style will generally elicit an answer even when the auditee doesn't want to or has been instructed not to answer. Conversely, a style that creates the perception of a threat or a cross-examination typically will not yield a positive result.

• *Providing too much detail or elaborating well beyond the auditor's request for information.* Auditees occasionally provide much more detail than the auditor desires when answering a question, whether unintentionally or intentionally. The auditor can and should politely keep the information flow on track.

• *Providing answer by others.* It is not uncommon for an auditor to ask a worker a question, and a nearby colleague or supervisor or the escort of the auditor will provide an answer. Auditors should get answers to questions from the individual to whom the question was directed.

• *Attempt to misdirect the auditor.* Auditors should be sensitive to the attempt by some auditees to manage the auditor—to show or tell the auditor what the employee wants to discuss rather than what the auditor wants to discuss.

• *Appeal to precedent.* Auditees will sometimes say something like, "I don't understand your concern. During the last audit the auditor said this was acceptable." Here the auditor should say something like, "I don't know those circumstances, but that's irrelevant. Let's discuss the requirements and the actual current situation."

• *Promote favorite crusades.* Occasionally an auditor is confronted with a reaction similar to: "Thank goodness you're looking into that. I have been trying to get them to fix it for six years." Sometimes this is a defense mechanism to point the auditor toward others or sometimes the auditee is looking for support for his own pet project. Sometimes the worker is correct. Auditors need to be very cautious in such circumstances.

• *Unbundle frustrations.* Occasionally auditors encounter employees who want to express their frustration with management or perhaps the entire enterprise, especially in times of reorganization or downsizing. Auditors should politely decline participating in such dialog unless it bears directly on the scope of the audit.

SUMMARY

This chapter presented the essential elements necessary for an individual to conduct an effective internal audit. It addressed the mechanics of auditing—the things an auditor must do to conduct an audit which include:

- Holding an opening meeting with the manager(s) of the area(s) to be audited

- Observing processes

- Observing final product, if applicable

- Asking questions

- Gathering objective evidence of the extent to which requirements are being met (and especially of any nonconformities noted)

- Keeping great notes

- Analyzing data

- Synthesizing all that is seen and heard and drawing conclusions

- Holding a closing meeting with manager(s) of the audited area

It also covered the human side of auditing—how an auditor should behave when conducting an audit. The personal characteristics discussed were:

- Interviewing skills

  - Listening skills

  - What to do when no documented procedures are available

  - Asking questions

  - Summarizing

- – Observing

- – Being respectful of auditees

- • Time management

- • Handling uncertainty, ambiguity, and conflict

- • Personal hygiene

The chapter concluded with a discussion of areas where auditors need to be particularly attentive—to ensure that they are being fair and impartial to the auditee and to ensure that they are not being managed or manipulated.

Collectively, the skill set described in this chapter, when diligently applied and practiced, will be sufficient to enable individuals to perform meaningful internal audits. The return to an organization on the investment in developing these audit skills can be substantial, and the personal satisfaction of the individual performing audits can be equally rewarding. When auditing is done right, everybody wins. The auditor, the auditee, and the organization all benefit.

10

Audit Reporting Phase

OUTPUT OF THE AUDIT

20 Auditing, like most of the activities mentioned in this text, is a process. As a process, the audit has inputs (requirements and field data), it has resources (mostly auditors), it has controls (common audit protocols and generally accepted practices), and it has an output (the report). In every audit, that report will take two forms: oral and written. As we move into the information age, it is becoming quite common for the written report to use virtual rather than paper media. The written report is more structured and formal than the oral report, but both contain common information.

COMPONENTS OF THE REPORT

Introductory Information

All communication must have a start. Auditing is no different. The receivers of the information may be quite close to the issues. They already know what was audited and why the audit was performed. Little introduction is needed. On the other hand, some of the readers know little or nothing about the audit subject matter. They will probably need quite a bit of background. To serve both parties, the introduction should be a paragraph or two at the most. It should restate the purpose and scope of the audit just performed. It should also identify the team leaders, by name, and the area or group audited, by function or location. A common guideline in auditing is to avoid names in the report, except for the auditors.

Overall Analysis of Control Systems

An auditor's principal task is to provide information to the various stakeholders on the overall controls associated with the system(s) just examined. This includes inputs, outputs, controls, and resources for the various interconnected processes. It is here that the bigger picture is drawn. Is the quality management system, as described in all the local documents, compliant with the external requirements for that organization? Is it being effectively implemented? Are there areas of inefficiency in need of management attention? Are there practices deserving of praise? This part of the report is about half a page when printed.

Finding Sheets

Next come the bad things. It is good practice to write up a brief summary of the problem areas, with finding sheets attached. Finding sheets are a way of documenting problems uncovered in an audit. It is common to create one finding sheet for each problem noted. A finding sheet shows the problem along with supporting objective evidence. Finding sheets can be helpful to clearly identify an issue to those that did not directly participate in the audit. They also help the auditee when considering corrective action alternatives.

Positive Practice Sheets

If activities deserving praise are seen during the audit, it is proper to describe these positive practices in the report. This is a change from the past, where auditors were instructed, "Don't say anything good. They may use it against us when we pressure them for improvement." Psychologists tell us that humans desire praise over punishment. Good deeds should be identified. As we discuss findings (below), remember that a positive practice is the opposite. Instead of bad facts and problems, we use good facts and controls.

HOW TO WRITE A FINDING

Definition of Finding

Over the many years of auditing, starting with the external financial accounting auditors and progressing to today's quality auditors, the term *finding* continues to be used. It comes from the legal term *finding of fact.* These are statements presented to a judge and designed to build a case either for or against a defendant. In the same manner, today's auditors use the term to convince stakeholders that something needs attention.

ISO 9000:2000, the fundamentals and vocabulary standard, gives us the definition:

3.9.5 *audit findings:* results of the evaluation of the collected *audit evidence* (3.9.4) against *audit criteria* (3.9.3). NOTE: Audit findings can indicate either conformity or nonconformity with audit criteria, or opportunities for improvement.

Source: ANSI/ISO/ASQ Q9000-2000. Used by permission.

This definition has limited usefulness, in that it was written for an international audience where some cultures use the term for both good and bad things. Most organizations use the term in a negative manner, whether for quality, environmental, or financial auditing. We will follow that common convention and use the term for nonconforming circumstances.

Assemble All Data

A *finding* is the output of an evaluation process. Inputs to that process are audit evidence (field data) and audit criteria (requirements).

The requirements are generally quite clear for most audits and are defined in the audit preparation steps, described earlier. The audit evidence can get quite messy during the data-gathering steps. Even though the team meetings and pauses for reflection help to add some order to the chaos, it is still necessary to define and clarify the many good and bad facts gathered during the course of the audit.

Our desire at this point is to develop a master list of facts. These statements of fact, whether good or bad, used to be called *observations.* As with many other quality audit concepts, the term came from external financial accounting auditors. Unfortunately, the term *observation* has lost its original meaning over the years, so we will continue to use the word fact. By design, these facts must be absolutely truthful and can contain no judgment other than "good" or "bad." By this we mean the fact either supports implementation of the criterion being evaluated (good) or it shows the criterion is not being implemented (bad). Success of the entire audit rests on the reader's ability to accept these facts as the truth.

As the audit progresses, various team members will be capturing data in their field notes and work papers. As stated earlier, these can be quite messy. These field notes must be evaluated and processed during the last team meeting, usually held a few hours before the exit or closing meeting. Under guidance of the team leader, auditors go through their notes and pick out the good and bad facts. The team leader captures these on two master lists: good and bad.

These two lists represent the accumulated facts from the audit. Other than "good" or "bad" categories, auditors should try not to do any sorting or filtering of the data yet. This is a transfer of raw data from the individual field notes.

Analyze and Sort the Data

The team has now agreed on the individual facts for:

- Truthfulness

- Objectivity

- Application to the audit scope

- Ability to communicate with all stakeholders

It is time to begin the sorting and analyzing. Figure 10.1 illustrates the analysis process. From the accumulated data, team members will propose problem statements (for bad facts) or affirmation statements (for good facts). Thinking back to the objectives of the audit and the controls being examined, the auditors address the question, "Is this being done? If not, can I prove it?" Requirements not met will eventually become findings.

The idea is to take the chaos of data and make some sense of it. Group the data into problem categories. If a fact relates to a problem, place it on that pile. If the fact relates to several problems, as will often happen, replicate it and place it on all the associated problem piles.

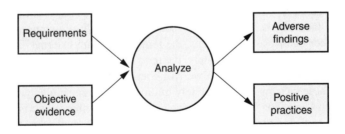

Figure 10.1 Analyze the data.

Develop the Problem Statement

 It is at this point where audit differs from inspection. Rather than report a punch list of bad data, auditors must process the data and form *subjective* opinions. A problem (or affirmation) statement will always be an opinion. That statement must always be supported by facts if it is to be accepted by the various stakeholders.

Develop the Consequences (Pain) of the Problem

For years, auditors have been bearers of bad news. One approach is to just state the problem and leave it up to others to determine the significance of that problem. This leaves the auditors totally free of the consequences of the report. They are free to be as nasty as they want to be. Sometimes, management desires this approach. They want the auditors to find any possible problem or nonconformity before the outside regulators, registrars, or customers. "Just give me the facts. I will determine if they need attention." While this approach has merit in some situations, it can be most frustrating for the internal auditors. They report the same condition on each audit, yet nothing is changed. Perhaps the time has come to provide management with an incentive.

If we can show the business consequences to the organization of a detected problem, managers are more apt to take notice. If they take notice, perhaps the system will be changed to keep the problem from recurring. This is exactly the philosophy of *continual improvement* expressed in ISO 9001:2000. Improve on the systems and processes to keep problems from recurring.

Using the same approach, auditors can even use business consequences of *potential* problems to drive continual improvement. Of course, this is much more difficult, as the data don't show an actual event yet. So the business consequences are much more difficult to predict. Uncovering potential problems as an objective of internal audits is one reason why internal auditors need to be bright and very capable individuals with the ability to think creatively. Internal auditing is not a job for mindless plodders.

Internal auditors have a great advantage in that they have access to data that outsiders may find difficult or impossible to obtain. It takes effort, but the data are there for harvesting by the internal auditors.

Organizational consequences should always address the big three: cost, product realization, and risk.

All organizations, whether manufacturing, government, or nonprofit, strive to lower the costs of producing goods and services. This is one of the reasons for interest in Six Sigma and lean manufacturing approaches.

Squeeze out every bit of waste and inefficiency to lower costs and increase customer satisfaction.

The time it takes to deliver goods and services is an important business driver. If our product realization methods are sound and working at optimal speed, we can meet our business commitments or even become best of class in the market. If not, the enterprise suffers.

Finally, all organizations experience risk. Risks must be minimized and sometimes mitigated for the organization to survive. Operational auditors, working for the board of directors or top management of a firm, will examine the potential for waste, fraud, and abuse. They examine the protection of assets from exposure to loss. Internal quality auditors should examine these same issues. If regulators shut down an organization, efficient production no longer matters.

If management and other stakeholders can see the business consequences of identified problems, they are much more likely to desire change. After all, that's the job of management—to effectively provide and direct resources to get the job done. If something is standing in the way, it should be removed.

A finding statement can take one of three forms:

1. Objective statement of the deficiency

2. Subjective statement of the problem, in business language

3. Subjective cause-and-effect statement, showing the problem and its business consequences

Whichever approach is used, the internal auditors have moved beyond the inspection role of reporting go and no-go. They have processed the data into something meaningful to management.

List Facts under the Finding Statement

Once the finding statement is written, each of the bad facts is listed underneath to show the supporting evidence. The desire is to get the reader to see the same facts and draw the same conclusions—that the control is not defined, implemented, or working, and here are the facts to prove it. Often, it is desirable to state the specific requirement along with the individual factual deficiency. This shows the factual basis for the nonconforming data.

Here are some examples of objective evidence statements:

- Quality procedure QP 1 requires quarterly management review. Only three reviews were held in the prior calendar year.

- Design procedure requires at least one design review. The file for project DEV2 contains no objective evidence of a design review being conducted.

- Service delivery work instruction SDWI3 requires the loan officer to solicit customer satisfaction comments at the conclusion of an applicant interview and to note comments or no comments in the LDB database. No comments were entered for two of five loan officers.

HOW TO WRITE A POSITIVE PRACTICE

Definition of Positive Practice

As noted above, the definition of *finding* may indicate compliance or noncompliance. Because most organizations use the term in a negative way, to show noncompliance, there is a need to use a different word when referring to good things. Within the last decade, the term *positive practice* arose for use in affirming that a control is defined, being implemented, and working.[1] A *positive practice* is the opposite of a *finding*. Instead of using facts showing noncompliance, a positive practice uses facts showing compliance.

Not all organizations will report positive practices. The idea of auditors saying something good is quite unsettling to some. It goes against the many years of audits only reporting problems and nonconformity. "No news is good news," was often the desired outcome. Even today, it is common (although not desirable) to avoid sending any report to a supplier who received no adverse findings.

For those organizations wishing to use audits to reinforce good performance, the positive practice is an effective tool. It is used to emphasize an especially effective method of controlling an operation. It may also be used to promote a practice across the organization, by showing other groups how well it works.

The *positive practice* is not used to report compliance. Rather, it is used to report higher-than-required performance.

Assemble All (Good!) Data

As with the adverse finding, the first step is to assemble all facts demonstrating compliance. This is not yet the time to sort and filter.

Analyze and Sort the Good Data

In examining the list of "good" facts, is there a control method or approach that seems to work especially well? Is there evidence to show strong understanding and support of that control throughout the organization? As before, the data are grouped into piles associated with the observed excellence. Generally, there will only be one or two such groupings.

Develop a Summary Statement of the Good Control Seen

 Now prepare a brief statement of the data-supported positive practice. The statement should show how the practice contributes to the organization's goals and business values. Here are some examples:

- There is a requirement for the supervisor to analyze final test data. The supervisor not only computed averages for test parameters, and performed Pareto analysis of out-of-spec results, but she calculated the cost impact of the test failures and presented justification in financial terms for a new piece of production equipment to reduce test failures.

- There is a requirement in the Customer Call Center to answer 95 percent of all customer calls within three rings. The supervisor constructed a run chart of response times and instituted process changes to improve response times so that 98 percent of all customer calls were answered in two rings.

List Good Facts under the Summary Statement

As with the adverse finding, list the positive facts under the positive statement. The form for noting positive practices can vary widely. Some examples include:

Quality objectives have been fully deployed through a system of performance agreements and personnel have a clear understanding of their roles in accomplishing them.

1. Key goals are communicated to the organization through a business planning and review process and through monthly luncheons, monthly Quality Council meetings, and other informal means.

2. Each functional head and each process owner has specific agreed-upon objectives that are linked directly to the organization's overall quality objectives.

3. Discussions with over fifty personnel revealed that each clearly understood his or her role in meeting process and functional quality objectives.

The organization has been successful in achieving improvements in customer satisfaction and a reduction in internal costs of rework by using analytical techniques.

1. Processes are measured and each key process has targets that relate to customer expectations.

2. Each of the ten key production processes has been improved over the past two years. Improvements have included a 50 percent reduction in rework cost, a 20 percent increase in process throughput, a 35 percent reduction in equipment downtime, and a 45 percent increase in customer satisfaction scores on customer satisfaction surveys.

3. Over the past 18 months, the operation's sales have increased by 25 percent and operating margins are up 10 percent.

The organization has become a benchmark within the company in the economical application of the preventive action concept. Over the past two years, the organization has:

1. Institutionalized the use of risk analysis and failure mode and effects analysis (FMEA) to define risks and prioritize actions.

2. Focused the effort on preventing machine downtime and process failures to meet quality requirements. Unscheduled downtime this year is about 50 percent lower than in each of the past five years while production volumes are up substantially. Customer returns are also down 45 percent.

Need to State an Overall Analysis

Another difference between internal and external auditors is the desire for a subjective opinion of strengths and weaknesses. This is not always done in an external audit by a regulator, registrar, or even a customer. Some would even argue that such an opinion is contrary to the objectives of an external audit. However, when auditing internally, such an opinion is highly desirable.

The various stakeholders expect the auditors to provide judgment and analysis. An exception would be when the purpose of the audit is to determine compliance of an operation to a given set of rules only. Otherwise, auditors are expected to add more to the analysis.

"Is the enterprise under control?" is a fair question. What are the strengths and weaknesses uncovered during the course of the audit? Is there reasonable assurance that the organization will continue to function effectively into the future? One of the great strengths of the internal audit is to take existing data and project them into the future.

From all the accumulated evidence, thoughts, and discussions, the team should prepare a one- or two-paragraph analysis of the overall effectiveness of those portions of the quality management system just audited. This is highly subjective and written for senior management. The analysis (and accompanying findings and positive practices) will become valuable input to the management review required by clause 5.6 of ISO 9001:2000.

During the transition to value-added internal auditing, there comes a time when senior management will build up sufficient trust in the audit program to ask for advice. Such *opportunities for improvement* are a great way to tap the collective wisdom of the audit staff. In a way, this is a form of internal consulting, but presented in the form of items or areas for management to consider, rather than as directives. As long as the suggestions are not specific how-to directions on accomplishing a task (that is the supervisor's job), they should be positively received by both the area supervision and by management. In addition to the overall analysis, an additional paragraph or two on areas for improvement may be quite desirable.

DELIVERY OF ORAL REPORT (EXIT MEETING)

As discussed in the previous chapter, an exit meeting is held with the auditee to present the report and resolve any misunderstandings. After the team has met to develop any finding or positive practice sheets, and to craft the overall analysis, it is *showtime*.

It is best to keep the exit meeting small. This minimizes the meeting room space hassle and it also keeps the potential for arguments down. As mentioned in chapter 2, the principle of *no secrets* will go a long way in reducing arguments. However, there are times when internal communications between the auditee staff are less than optimal. Some just don't get the word or others won't communicate facts for fear of retaliation. Regardless, there's always a possibility for arguing at the exit meeting. Keep focused on the audit results and back up your opinions with objective evidence and the arguments will be less stressful.

It is good practice for the team leader to conduct the exit meeting. This keeps the meeting moving and minimizes discrepancies between team members. There are four steps to perform:

1. *Present the background information.* What was audited and why was it examined? Where did you focus your time and attention? What groups did you talk to? Remember to refer to groups or areas rather than specific individuals.

2. *Present the overall analysis of the audited area.* This is the big picture.

3. *Present a summary of each finding and positive practice.* Some like to cover findings first and some like to do them last. Use your own personal preference. If allowed by the culture of your firm, pass out your draft finding sheets at this point. Make sure people know they are drafts and subject to editorial review by the audit boss. By passing out these sheets at the exit meeting, the internal auditors emphasize trust, cooperation, and service to others. You should probably not require the auditee to sign these sheets, as it might be perceived as a coerced confession of guilt.

4. *If problems are uncovered, review the process used for corrective action.* This is discussed in greater detail in the next chapter. Make sure the auditees understand the need for response and the mechanism that will be used to receive, evaluate, and monitor those responses. Blank forms are good here. They act as props when explaining the response process.

DELIVERY OF WRITTEN REPORT

The written report, whether paper or electronic, is the formal delivery of the information presented at the exit meeting. It is developed by the team and delivered to the audit boss by the team leader.

The audit report is the record of the audit. It should contain or refer to the following:

- Purpose, scope, and criteria of the audit
- Audit objectives

- Identification of the auditors and auditee (remember to avoid names, except for the audit team)

- Dates and places where evidence was gathered

- Overall conclusions

- Findings and positive practices

The first three items above are the background information presented at the exit meeting. The overall conclusions, plus any opportunities for improvement, are the written version of what was presented orally to the auditee. The findings and positive practices are generally summarized first, with the individual sheets attached to the report.

Some organizations desire a more complete, stand-alone package. In this case, ISO 19011:2002 recommends that you consider adding the additional material listed in Figure 10.2 to the report.

Most of these additional items are more applicable to very large and complex organizations or external audit programs rather than small organizations.

- Audit plan

- List of auditee representatives, should future meetings occur

- Summary of the audit process, including any uncertainties or obstacles that might reduce the reliability of the reported information

- Confirmation that the audit achieved its objectives

- Any areas within the audit scope but not covered

- Any unresolved differences of opinion

- Recommendations for improvement

- Any agreements on follow-up action plans

- Statement on confidentiality of the audit report and its information

- Distribution list for the audit report

Figure 10.2 Supplementary information to consider for audit reports.
Source: BSR/ISO/ASQ QE 19011-2002. Used by permission.

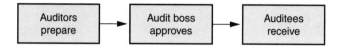

Figure 10.3   Delivery of the written report.

The written report should go through the audit boss, for transmittal to the auditee. Delivery of the report is illustrated in Figure 10.3. This gives management visibility and accountability to the audit program. Often, individual auditors participate on only one or two audits during an audit cycle (which is typically a year), while the audit boss usually has a degree of permanence. We will discuss in the next chapter how any adverse issues are subsequently tracked.

ENDNOTE

1. Dennis R. Arter, *Quality Audits for Improved Performance* (Milwaukee: ASQ Quality Press, 2002).

11

Audit Closure Phase

The last paragraph of ISO 9001:2000 clause 8.2.2 not only requires that the audits be planned and conducted but also that the managers of the area audited ". . . ensure that actions are taken without undue delay to eliminated detected nonconformities and their causes." It also requires that there be follow-up activities that ". . . include the verification of the actions taken and the reporting of verification results." The responsibility of this follow-up action is not specified.

There can be considerable debate over when an audit should be closed. Some organizations close the audit when the report is officially issued. Others do not close out an audit until after the completion and verification of corrective action. Some organizations involve auditors in this verification while others rely on the auditee. Let's review the options:

• *Close the audit as soon as the report is issued.* This reflects a purist's view and maintains strict independence of the auditor. This view is based on the idea that it avoids all possible criticisms that the auditor or the audit process has been engaged in consulting activities. But, of course, just because there is no indication of consulting activity in the audit report or subsequent records does not mean that it has not occurred. With this option, all activities subsequent to issue of the report are entrusted to other parts of the quality management system. For example, if corrective action is required on nonconformities, the auditee is generally required to meet all the requirements for corrective action, including verification. In some organizations, the verification activity may be done by another part of the organization such as a quality engineering department. While this option may represent the purest form of auditor independence, it has the potential dis-advantage of disengaging the auditor from the rest of the organization and may make the audit process appear to be a finger-pointing exercise.

• *Close the audit after all audit items have been transferred to another part of the quality management system.* This option keeps the auditor and audit boss engaged until the issues have been fully understood and docu-mented in detail. This is probably the most commonly used option.

• *Close the audit only after all actions have been completed and veri-fied.* This process involves the auditing group in the process until all prob-lems have been corrected and verified. This has the advantage of increasing auditors' involvement with auditees. Its major disadvantage is that it may give the auditee managers the perception that audit findings are the audit organization's problem rather than his or her own. With careful implemen-tation, this option can be implemented in a way that is effective and main-tains auditor independence. This option was common in the past but is seldom used now.

The authors consider it best to close out the audit report after required actions have been transferred to action request documents. Whatever com-bination of timing and responsibilities is selected, the documented audit program procedure should describe the closeout process and explain who is responsible for follow-up and verification.

TRANSFER OF AUDIT ISSUES TO ACTION REQUESTS

From a practical point of view, the auditor, the audit boss, supporting staff quality engineers, or the managers in the areas audited could prepare these documents. In any case, the audit program procedure should describe how it is done, who does it, and how the documents are reviewed for adequacy prior to issue. The action requests could be inputs to other parts of the qual-ity management system such as corrective action or preventive action. Alternatively, they could be documents that are an integral part of the audit program. The remainder of this chapter will assume that the audit report has been drafted, reviewed with the auditee during an exit meeting, and is being finalized for issue. All that remains is the transfer of audit findings and any other action items to other documents to drive the needed action.

It is useful to distinguish between three situations: (1) violations of requirements (that is, findings or nonconformities) or issues with effective-ness or efficiency, (2) potential problems (identified risks), and (3) process excellence or observed best practices. The distinction between nonconformity and opportunities for performance improvement is discussed in part I, chapter 4 and illustrated in Figure 4.1, page 44. This distinction was important during audit planning and as we conducted the audit. Now this distinction is critical.

In some cases, the corrective or preventive action may seem obvious. Great care is needed in these cases to ensure that the action request does not include personal opinions.

If the action request is not clear, not stated correctly, or is prescriptive, the chances of achieving the required actions are greatly diminished. The audit process should provide clear distinction between requests for corrective action, opportunities for preventive action, and other types of observations.

THREE SITUATIONS

Those who develop action requests need to clearly understand the difference between corrective action and preventive action. They also need to know what to do with audit items that represent "good" audit results. Let's review each of these three situations:

• A corrective action request (CAR—see ISO 9001:2000 clause 8.5.2) should be used when observations and evidence indicate there is a deviation from either a requirement or from a possible better state of performance. An example of a deviation from a requirement could be an activity that is not being carried out as required in the applicable documented procedure. An example of a deviation from possible better performance might be a process that is stable and operating as it always has but is not meeting its quality objectives. In either case, the cause of the deviation may or may not be known. If the cause is unknown, the auditee's corrective action process should include the use of problem-solving methods to determine the cause(s) of the deviation.

If the auditee knows the cause of the deviation, the necessary action may be obvious. In this case, the part of the problem-solving process concerning determination of cause is unnecessary but possible solutions must still be defined and decisions made as to what action to implement.

• If the audit evidence reveals a risk of future nonconformity or potential problems, a preventive action request is appropriate. Preventive action addresses potential causes of problems or nonconformities that have not yet occurred. The study of such situations is generally more complex than the study required to solve known problems, and usually requires the use of different tools. In such cases, the problem-solving process may lead to confusion, and other tools, such as failure mode and effects analysis (FMEA), risk analysis, and cost–benefit analysis may be needed.

• When the audit observations and evidence indicate superior process performance, there may be an opportunity to deploy the knowledge gained to other processes or parts of the organization using a "best observed practices" process. This situation is different from either of the other two situations described, generally requiring a clear determination of how the "best practice" operates and a full demonstration of how it achieves superior results.

Achieving improvements through corrective action may involve more than one stage. In fact, some organizations define two (or more) levels of corrective action. The first level may involve implementing corrective action on the immediately apparent cause of a problem. The second level may address deeper underlying causes that can only be determined after analysis.

Deployment of best-observed practices may require significant top management involvement. Proper documentation of the situation is critical to ensure that the opportunities are clearly presented and the potential value of taking action is demonstrated.

DEVELOPMENT OF CORRECTIVE ACTION REQUESTS FROM THE AUDIT REPORT

For identified nonconformities and problems with efficiency it is appropriate to transfer the findings to corrective action requests (CARs). Remember, the people who act on the CARs may not have been involved in the audit. It is critical to capture not only what the problem is, but also the facts and supporting evidence used to write the original findings. Supporting the facts with actual measurements of part conformity (ppm, percent defective, and so on), process performance, or other indicators of the problem, will promote better understanding. Simply stating conclusions is not sufficient. A full statement of the issues, conclusions, opportunities for improvement, and supporting evidence is necessary for two reasons:

• Those who will take corrective action need to fully grasp where the problem was found, the exact nature of the problem, the process and people involved, and the reasons for the auditor's conclusions.

• It emphasizes to decision-makers the benefit that will occur if the problem is solved. The CARs should emphasize this opportunity. This approach focuses on the positive aspects of the situation without sugar-coating them—opportunities may be easier to deal with than problems. More importantly, it serves to convince managers of the magnitude of the opportunity so they are more likely to take action.

Careful development of the CARs is the responsibility of the auditor and the audit boss. If it is not done correctly, the credibility of the whole audit process suffers. Each CAR should be carefully reviewed to ensure it is complete but avoids "finger-pointing" or prescribing solutions.

CORRECTING IDENTIFIED NONCONFORMITIES OR PROBLEMS

Requests for corrective action are based on nonconformities or other problems identified in the audit. The corrective action process addresses the cause(s) of these problems. The specific nonconformities are merely evidence that the cause(s) need to be determined and corrected. It is also necessary that the organization's system provide for correction of the specific items that were found to be nonconforming. Correction does not deal with causes but rather addresses the specific nonconforming item itself.

THE CORRECTIVE ACTION PROCESS

Corrective action is action taken to eliminate the cause(s) of problems or nonconformities. The audit program should assign responsibility for corrective action to the managers of the audited areas, not to the auditor. It is the responsibility of these managers to develop a corrective action plan. In fact, the entire corrective action process is the responsibility of these managers. We will not deal with the corrective action process in detail but some key parts of the process are:

• *Prioritization of actions.* It is the responsibility of the managers of the areas audited to prioritize these actions and to fit them in with all of the other work they must accomplish. Sometimes, it is urgent that actions be taken quickly. Action planning and timing should suit the situation.

• *Evaluating the need to take action.* Along with prioritization, there needs to be an evaluation of whether action should be taken at all. There are cases where minor audit findings can have relatively small impacts on the organization and no effect on its customers. In such cases, it may be more important to take action on other issues. This does not mean that the auditee arbitrarily decides to take no action because he or she doesn't want to or because it would require extra work. Rather, it means a mature judgment is made that other activities are much more important.

• *Deciding what to do if corrective action is obvious.* Sometimes it is obvious what action needs to be taken. In this case, the cause of the non-conformity or problem may or may not be known. But the solution is known so there is no need to spend effort in finding the cause. In such cases, the management of the area must make a decision to implement the needed change. The decision can be documented on the CARs and should include the timing of the changes, how to measure results, and any necessary implementation plans.

• *Using problem-solving techniques if cause needs to be determined.* Some nonconformities involve a situation in which the managers of the area being audited do not know how to correct the problem. In this situation, the cause may actually be known but its remedy may not be clear. In other cases the managers may not know the cause. In this situation, the manager needs to use problem-solving methods to determine the cause (if it is unknown), develop possible solutions, evaluate those possible solutions, and implement the ones that make sense.

• *Measuring the results of the actions taken.* If action is worth taking, it is worth measuring the results. Often audit programs demand only that the finding not be repeated on subsequent audits. Actually, it should be the responsibility of the auditee managers to know that the actions they have taken have been effective in reducing the incidence of, or eliminating the identified problem. The best way for these managers to know that they have had this impact is for them to measure the results. Well-written audit reports and CARs that include measurements of performance can help auditees understand how to measure their improvements.

DEVELOPMENT OF PREVENTIVE ACTION REQUESTS FROM THE AUDIT REPORT

Corrective action requests need to clearly describe the nature of the nonconformity or problem. When potential problems are identified, an adequate description is even more crucial. In such cases the auditor has concluded that the potential exists for a nonconformity or other problem to happen in the future. The auditee may actually have plenty of problems in the present! While it is intuitively obvious that preventing problems from ever occurring in the first place is better than correcting their causes after they have happened, operating personnel often feel that they do not have the time or resources to do the work required for prevention. In writing preventive action requests, the auditor and the audit boss need to carefully consider how they would feel if asked to prevent the potential problems cited in the audit report. The auditor and the audit boss must recognize that there are an infinite number of possible things to prevent. This means that recommendations for preventive action should be made only in cases where the auditor and the audit boss can convince themselves of their potential value.

In the preparation of preventive action requests, auditors should consider:

• *Capturing the facts, risks, and conclusions.* It is much easier to record what has already happened than it is to describe why a potential problem may occur in the future. There are several questions that should be answered during the drafting of each preventive action request. First, what is the potential future failure? Second, what is the probability that this potential failure will occur? Third, what effects would this potential failure have if it were to occur? Fourth, what is the likelihood that the organization's processes would catch the failure before any serious effect occurs? Answering these questions is a means of quantifying the risks associated with a potential failure, nonconformity, or problem.

• *Emphasis on the opportunity.* The preventive action request should emphasize why it is important to install preventive measures in this specific case. It is not appropriate for the auditor or the audit boss to actually conduct a cost–benefit analysis in such situations (because this would require identification of what preventive action steps to take), but it is normally best to quantify the risk in financial terms.

THE PREVENTIVE ACTION PROCESS

As with corrective action, the preventive action process is the responsibility of managers in the audited area. While it is important to plan for corrective actions, planning for prevention is critical. This planning should consider:

• *Prioritization of actions.* The risk may be so significant that some preventive measures need to be taken immediately. On the other hand, in most cases where the risk may be high, the probability of it occurring in the immediate future is not great. For this reason, preventive action requests may be relegated to the "back burner." But if the risk has been spelled out in clear terms and quantified financially, managers of the audited area are far more likely to put high priority on the item.

• *Action plans.* Action plans for corrective action tend to be simple when compared to those needed in projects related to preventive action. Often, preventive action requests require significant study to better understand the potential effects, develop possible prevention alternatives, determine the best alternatives, and implement them. All this must be carefully planned. It is not uncommon for such projects to involve capital expenditures or product redesign. In such cases, the capital expenditure or design project may need to be included in a future year's plan. If the risk is great and the probability of occurrence high, it may be necessary to obtain high-level approval of emergency funding. All of this means that there may be a need for significant top management involvement in the planning of preventive actions.

• *Determining potential causes and their potential effects.* A tool like FMEA is appropriate for determining potential causes, their potential effects, and to prioritize them. Often, the original preventive action request will describe the potential failure mode. Since preventive actions can be expensive to implement, it should not be assumed that the failure mode discussed in the preventive action request is the only one or even the most important.

• *Evaluating the risk and determining what action, if any, to take.* A key part of the plan is evaluating the risk to determine whether there's even a need for change. The FMEA technique and cost–benefit analysis can also provide insight into the risks and possible alternatives. Once these analyses have been completed, it should be clear which actions should be taken, if any.

• *Implementation planning.* Typically, preventive actions require implementation planning to ensure they are installed and work properly. This needs to include a plan for testing the preventive action to ensure it will actually work.

• *Measuring the results of the actions taken.* Measuring results of preventive action generally involves conducting tests to ensure the preventive measure will work. This may involve testing the preventive measure by introducing known defects into the process or by other means to ensure that the preventive process change actually works.

While the steps appear to be similar to those specified previously for corrective action, it is important to understand that the differences are actually quite significant. This is particularly true when one considers the planning required in the testing and possible product reverification and revalidation that may be necessary to ensure successful implementation.

DOCUMENTING EXAMPLES OF EXCELLENCE OR BEST PRACTICES FROM THE AUDIT REPORT

Audits discover good practices as well as bad, and audit reports should include "good" items. If results are good, the audit report needs to include sufficient information to justify that conclusion. Where such good items are included to demonstrate that processes conform to requirements and are meeting required targets, discussion in the audit report itself may be sufficient to recognize that achievement. Areas that get satisfactory audit results can easily be recognized in the organization's newsletter or other publication. This may be particularly appropriate for areas that have consistently good audit results over time.

Sometimes an audit report describes situations, activities, or even whole processes that exhibit excellence in terms of results. Often such items find their way into the audit report but not beyond. Demonstrated excellence should not be lost; it should be studied and, if appropriate, deployed to other parts of the organization. Some organizations have extensive "best practices" processes and databases to facilitate the sharing of such examples of excellence. In some organizations, this is a part of a knowledge management process that may include other components such as competitive benchmarking. Organizations that do not have a best practices or knowledge management process may want to create a mechanism to share or deploy such knowledge. It is not uncommon for the audit boss to take the lead in this. After all, auditors commonly observe not only the worst practices in the organization but also the best.

We will not attempt to provide a complete description of a process for deploying best practices. We will describe how an audit program can include a simple mechanism for documenting and distributing best practices.

The Audit Boss's Role

Before creating a process for documenting and deploying best practices observed during audits, the audit boss should obtain top management concurrence with an approach to address the subject. Nothing can be more frustrating than spending time on documenting a practice only to discover that it is never deployed to other parts of the organization. The cultures within some organizations are such that just issuing a document to describe an excellent practice results in instant rejection. This may be because of the typical "not invented here" attitude or it may be due to the egos of competing top managers. It is important, therefore, for the audit boss to achieve consensus among the top management group that they will ensure honest consideration of better ideas from other parts of the organization. In the absence of such a consensus, deployment of best practices beyond the part of the organization in which they were observed is not likely. Caution is needed when deciding which items to document. If the observed excellent results are caused by normal variation (such as an upswing in the business cycle), it is not prudent to include the item. If the results cannot be demonstrated as having been caused by the process, there is no value in documenting the item as a best observed practice.

Documenting the Practice

Preparing corrective action requests and preventive action requests is largely a process of transferring the information from the audit report and the auditor's experiences to a form. In these cases, an auditor (without much input from the auditee) may easily prepare the items. Documenting best practices is more complicated. The auditor, in the course of the audit, normally does not have sufficient time to completely map out the process so that it is clear why superior results are being achieved. In fact, when a good process is observed, the auditor's job is to move on to the next process! Seldom do auditors have sufficient time to completely document excellence. If this documentation is to be complete, it is probably necessary to involve personnel from the audited organization in preparing it.

 This documentation needs to describe the results obtained, explain why these results are excellent, and explain how the process caused the excellent results to occur. Often the reasons for excellence are very complex and may be as dependent on work environment, individual performance of workers, technology, or other supporting factors as they are on the core process itself. For effective transfer of the best observed practice to other parts of the organization, these key factors must be learned in those other parts of the organization. Part of this learning is facilitated by a well-written best observed practice document.

Deciding What, If Any, Deployment Action to Take

Sometimes distribution of a best practices report or its inclusion in the best practices database is all that is necessary. If the benefits of adapting the process throughout the organization are small, it may not be worthwhile to take any additional deployment action. On the other hand, if the best practice is a major innovation that could vastly improve organizational performance if it were used more commonly, additional action may be warranted. The audit boss could, for example, raise these issues as a part of the management review process via a recommendation that top management undertake a study to determine whether the practice should become a required organizationwide method. Such a review could include a cost–benefit analysis and an external benchmarking study. Such a universal deployment of a best practice normally needs to be a top management decision.

Team Approach to Process Deployment

For major process changes, some organizations find it beneficial to establish a team to conduct implementation planning and facilitate the change. The implementation of a best practice that involves major process change throughout the organization is generally accomplished by following this approach.

Providing Recognition

Involvement of auditee personnel in documenting best practices is a mechanism for recognition. Once the process has been documented, the best practices report can be distributed or placed in a database for others in the organization to use. The audit boss can ensure that best practices documented during audits are discussed with top management during management reviews. The organization's newsletter can be used to point out superior results in processes and people behind them. In any event, care should be taken to give credit to the organization that demonstrated the best practice, not the auditor!

THE AUDIT BOSS'S RESPONSIBILITY FOR FOLLOW-UP

Basic follow-up to ensure that actions are taken rests with the management of the organizations that have been audited. But the audit boss needs to make certain that these other managers are fulfilling their role. The audit boss can ask for reports of actions that are being taken, project plans, and measured results. The management review process can also be used to establish a system in which each corrective action request, preventive action request, and documented best practice is reported on during the management review process. If this is done, issues related to inadequate action or long-delayed action can be discussed with top managers, and resources reallocated or other action taken to resolve them.

A well-designed corrective and preventive actions database can help the audit boss monitor or progress on required actions.

Maintaining Files of Reports and Data to Be Used in Planning Future Audits

The audit boss needs to maintain the audit files. In fact, there should be one set of centralized audit files and the audit boss should not allow individual auditors to keep these records. These records should include as a minimum:

1. Audit schedules

2. Audit plans

3. Auditors working papers

4. Audit reports

5. Corrective action requests, preventive action requests, and documented best practices

6. Reports or records of feedback from auditees on actions taken

These records serve as evidence that the audit program is functioning effectively. But that is only one reason for their maintenance. A primary purpose of these records is to aid in planning future audits. It is insufficient to have a fixed audit schedule that requires auditing of each part of the organization at predetermined intervals. The audit schedule and even the type of audit conducted should take into account the results of prior audit experience.

12
Reinventing the Audit Process

In the early stages of implementing the quality management system, auditing is often the only road to system improvement. The audit process is focused primarily on achieving conformity and process stability. This focus is appropriate with a new system. The audit program adds value by providing a means to measure system stability and conformity, a stimulus to improve, and a means to verify that improved stability and conformity have been achieved.

SIGNS OF QMS MATURITY

As the processes of the quality management system stabilize, the system matures. As the system matures, top managers begin to see audit results improve dramatically. No longer do they hear about major disconnects between actual performance and the written procedures and charted processes. Auditing may become a simple task of verifying ongoing conformity. When this happens, the audit program is in danger. There are typical signs that appear when this begins to happen:

- A reduction in the number and significance of audit findings related to failures to conform with procedures or process requirements

- Fewer corrective actions taken on audit-related issues

- Apparent loss of interest by top managers in audit results

- Comments by top managers related to a perceived need to reduce resources expended in auditing

It may take several years for these signs to appear but they are quite normal. The audit boss needs to recognize when conditions have changed. The audit program needs to change with those different conditions. If the audit processes are not refocused, it is likely that top management support for the audit program will decline, and audit resources may be diverted to other activities that have a greater potential for adding value. Sometimes, improving the use and analysis of audit data and information can revitalize the audit program. In other cases it is necessary to reinvent the audit program!

REEVALUATE YOUR USE OF AUDIT DATA

The first step for the audit boss to take is to reassess how audit information is being used. Early in their development, audit programs tend to focus on individual audit findings that arise in the various processes or functions of the organization. This narrow focus is often needed to achieve process stability. On the other hand, a narrow focus may cause the audit program to miss significant opportunities for cross-functional and systemwide improvements. This means the audit boss needs to return to part II, chapter 7 and rethink how audit data are analyzed and used.

RE-CHARTER THE AUDIT PROGRAM

If the organization is doing a good job of using audit data and information, there is likely a need to reassess the audit program objectives. This subject was reviewed in detail in part I, chapter 4. Often, the initial assessment of audit program purpose results in the conclusion that the program should focus on conformity of the quality management system to ISO 9001. In fact, this may be a good initial decision, but for the audit program to continue as a value-adding activity, it may need to shift its focus toward identification of opportunities for improving performance. The audit boss who is in this situation should engage top managers in a reassessment of the audit program's basic purpose.

This reassessment should lead to a re-chartering of the audit program. Development of the charter was discussed in part II, chapter 5.

DON'T FORGET THE BASIC PRINCIPLES

As conditions change there may be a temptation to forego some of the auditing principles and ethics that were reviewed in part I, chapter 1 and part II, chapter 6. It is the audit boss's job to resist this temptation. Auditing must always and forever be conducted in a professional and ethical manner.

THE AUDIT BOSS NEEDS TO ACT

The bottom line is that the audit boss needs to be proactive in managing the health of the audit program. As the quality system matures, the audit program needs to change. This is illustrated in Figure 12.1 which shows that auditing shifts from determining how well the quality management sysem conforms to finding opportunities to improve performance. If the audit boss is clever and resourceful, the audit program can remain a valuable tool for improving performance.

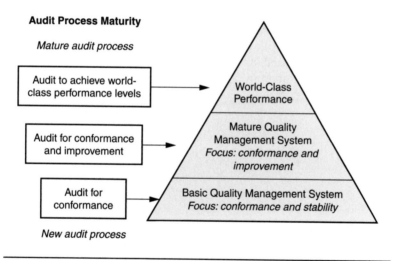

Figure 12.1 The quality audit hierarchy.

Part IV

Aids for Audit Program Implementation

INTRODUCTION

Parts I through III provided a discussion of auditing, development of the audit program, audit processes, and actually conducting audits. Part IV supplements the text of parts I through III with tools (worksheets and forms), checklists, and questions that should help the audit boss develop and manage the audit program. The purpose for including this material is to cause the organization and the audit boss to think about the audit program development, its processes, and the people associated with the audit program.

13

Tools, Checklists, and Questions

Worksheets are provided to illustrate many of the thought processes discussed in the text of parts I through III. They may be used as is or modified as appropriate for individual applications. Once developed and filled in, the worksheets could be retained as evidence that the organization has thought through the issues involved, but there is no intent to imply that there is a requirement in ISO 9001:2000 to document all of the material provided in the worksheets.

Forms are provided for some applications where they are normally employed in quality management system auditing. No attempt has been made to include every form that might be appropriate in your circumstances, nor does the inclusion of a form or data on a form imply that this specific data, form, or format is a requirement for meeting ISO 9001:2000 internal audit requirements. Rather, it is intended that the forms included stimulate the audit boss to think about the types and formats of forms used in the organization's internal quality audit program. And remember that forms should be designed to meet the needs of the organization, not vice versa.

Checklists are included to help the audit boss and auditors ensure that they don't forget to accomplish tasks that are necessary to the successful operation of the audit program.

This part also includes a set of audit questions arranged by ISO 9001:2000 clause number. These questions are derived from the "Audit questions for compliance" given in *ISO 9001:2000 Explained*, Second Edition, by Charles A. Cianfrani, Joseph J. Tsiakals, and John E. (Jack) West, and published by ASQ Quality Press. These questions are provided to give the audit boss an understanding of the depth and breadth of the issues that may arise in auditing a quality management system that is designed to meet the ISO 9001:2000 requirements.

Users are encouraged to modify the items included in part IV to suit their own needs:

- Forms may be modified to show a company logo or to add or delete information to be recorded to suit the individual application.

- The worksheets can be used as is or modified to suit the organization's needs.

- The questions are provided as reference material and must be tailored during the audit planning process to ensure that the auditors are able to gather the necessary audit information.

ITEM 1 WORKSHEET—AUDIT APPROACHES (HORIZONTAL, VERTICAL, COMBINATION OF HORIZONTAL AND VERTICAL)

Step 1. Identify QMS Processes and Functions (Departments) Involved

Function			Top management	Sales	Product development	Production	QA	Others	
	Function analysis →								
Process									
		Process analysis ↓							
Customer focus and satisfaction			P	I	I	S	S		
Order entry			S	P	I	S	I		
Design and development			S		P	S	I		
Human resource development			I	I	I	I	I		
Others									

Involvement Code: P—Primary responsibility; I—Important involvement; S—Somewhat involved

Step 2. Analyze Available Data For Each Function and Each Process

- Data by function
    - Functional performance data
    - Prior audit data
    - Importance of function
- Data by process
    - Process performance data
    - Prior audit data
    - Importance of function

Answer the following questions:

Which processes are the most critical to success of the QMS?

Which processes offer the greatest opportunity for improvement of the QMS?

Which processes offer the greatest opportunity for performance improvement?

Which functions are most critical to the success of the QMS?

Which functions offer the greatest opportunity for performance improvement?

Which functions offer the greatest opportunity for improvement of the QMS?

Step 3. For each process and function, analyze the relative importance and potential to achieve improvements.

Function		Top management	Sales	Product development	Production	QA	Others	
	Function analysis →	C/L/L	I/L/L	C/H/H	C/M/H	H/L/L		
Process								
	Process analysis ↓							
Customer focus and satisfaction	C/L/H	P	I	I	S	S		
Order entry	I/L/L	S	P	I	S	I		
Design and development	C/H/H	S		P	S	I		
Human resource development	I/L/H	I	I	I	I	I		
Others								

Involvement Code: P—Primary responsibility; I—Important involvement; S—Somewhat involved.

Process and Functional Analysis:
  • Importance: C—Critical; N—Not critical.
  • Potential to improve the QMS: H—High; M—Medium; L—Low.
  • Potential to improve performance: H—High; M—Medium; L—Low.

Step 4. Considering resources required for functional (vertical) or horizontal auditing, and the other information, decide on a strategy.

> *In the example above, you might choose to audit human resource development horizontally and all of the others vertically by function.*

Horizontal or vertical:

> Which functions will you audit vertically?

> Which processes will you audit horizontally?

Scheduling:

> In scheduling audits, which functions will you audit most frequently?

> In scheduling audits, which functions will you audit least frequently?

> In scheduling audits, which processes will you audit most frequently?

> In scheduling audits, which processes will you audit least frequently?

ITEM 2 WORKSHEET—AUDIT OBJECTIVES AND CRITERIA

Determination of objectives:

Possible objectives	1*	2*	3*	Audit criteria
Requirements-related objectives:				
1				Define the documents that you will audit against.
2				
Efficiency objectives				
1				Define the performance criteria and sources thereof.
2				
Risk-finding objectives				
1				Define the criteria to be used in determining extent of risk.
2				

* The audit needs to pursue this item in this way:

1. Deep process study needed (consider audit resources and time required)

2. Consider this aspect to be a key part of the audit

3. Do not look for this during the audit

Audit Objectives, Scope, and Team

Audit Objectives

> *From the list of objectives, write a simple, clear statement of the objective for the audit. A short statement followed by bullets is suggested.*

Audit Scope

> *From the list of objectives, write a simple, clear statement of the scope for the audit. A short statement followed by bullets is suggested.*

Audit Team Requirements and Selection

Special requirements for audit team leader	Team leader for the audit
Define any special requirements that the audit team leader should have to conduct this specific audit.	*List the name of the team leader selected to conduct this audit.*
Special requirements for audit team members	Audit team members
Define any special requirements that the audit team leader should have to conduct this specific audit.	*List the audit team members. Show which team members meet each defined special requirement.*

ITEM 3 WORKSHEET—AUDIT PROGRAM CHARTER

Who should charter the audit program?	What action is needed to obtain their commitment?
•	•
•	•
•	•
What are the key reasons for having a sound internal quality audit program?	**What results should be achieved from the internal audit program?**
•	•
•	•
•	•
What options do we have for audit program resources?	**What are the advantages and disadvantages of each option?**
•	•
•	•
•	•
•	•

Write a draft charter for the audit program.

ITEM 4 CHECKLIST—ITEMS TO CONSIDER WHEN PREPARING AN INTERNAL AUDITING PROCEDURE

Does the procedure address:

- ❑ The objectives of the overall internal audit program
- ❑ Who "owns" the internal audit program
- ❑ A process for identification of processes to be audited
- ❑ Scheduling of individual audits to be performed
- ❑ Selection of the processes, areas, and functions to be audited
- ❑ Dissemination of an annual plan of what to audit
- ❑ Auditor selection and a process for determining who can audit what
- ❑ Responsibilities for planning and conducting audits
- ❑ Reporting of audit results
- ❑ Relationship of audit process to the corrective action process and to follow-up

Additional considerations:

The internal audit procedure does not have to be long or complex.

The procedure is generally "owned" by the audit boss.

ITEM 5 WORKSHEET—DEVELOPING AN OVERALL AUDIT SCHEDULE FOR AN ORGANIZATION

Area / Schedule	Product Design & Development	Corrective Action	Product Realization Process #1	Product Realization Process #2	Documentation	Etc. →
1Q	Auditor #1		Auditor #7		Audit Team #9	
2Q		Audit Team #2		Auditor #12		
3Q					Audit Team #3	
4Q		Audit Team #4				

1. List the activities to be audited across the top of the matrix:

   - Functional areas, for example, bank teller process or subassembly test

   - Organizationwide processes, for example, documentation, corrective action

2. List the time periods along the left side of the matrix.

3. Identify all the quality management systems processes and all the product realization processes to be audited for the audit period, for example, a year. There may be 40 processes or more to be audited depending on the size of the organization and the products or services provided.

4. Identify all auditors in the audit pool and any limitations on availability and capability (for example, Harry is only qualified to audit administrative processes).

5. Decide which processes can be audited by individual auditors and which processes will require a team.

6. Fill in the matrix by assigning auditors to all the processes to be audited in the desired time periods.

7. Be prepared to modify the matrix during the audit period as the plan progresses.

8. Maintain flexibility.

ITEM 6 CHECKLIST—AUDITOR CHARACTERISTICS

Characteristic qualifications to look for when evaluating and selecting personnel to perform internal audits:

❏ *Inquisitive nature.* An individual who wonders how things work may make a good auditor.

❏ *Oral communication skills.* Auditors must have the ability to ask clear, coherent questions.

❏ *Listening skills.* Active listening is a requirement for a good auditor.

❏ *Project and time management skills.* Auditors need to manage their time and conduct audits in a logical manner.

❏ *Ability to get along with people.* Argumentative individuals generally do not make good auditors.

❏ *Writing skills.* Auditors need to be able to write coherent and compelling reports that engender action.

❏ *Organizational skills.* Auditors need to handle volumes of paper and information and quickly separate the important from the trivial.

❏ *Flexibility.* Willing to look at new approaches and understand benefits (and risks).

ITEM 7 CHECKLIST—RESPONSIBILITIES OF AUDIT PERSONNEL

Audit Team Leaders

❑   Planning, organizing, and directing the audit

❑   Representing the team to the auditee and the audit boss

❑   Leading the team in reaching conclusions

❑   Preventing and resolving conflicts

❑   Preparing and completing the audit report

Team Members

❑   Preparing for their assignments

❑   Gathering data and forming conclusions

❑   Contributing to the audit report

Subject Matter Experts

❑   Advising the team on possible sources of data

❑   Gathering data within their specialty area

❑   Assisting in the analysis of data within their specialty area

❑   Contributing to the technical accuracy of the report

ITEM 8 CHECKLIST—TRAINING AND EXPERIENCE TO ENSURE AUDITOR COMPETENCE

❏ Formal training on ISO 9001:2000. Each auditor should have a good understanding of both the requirements of ISO 9001:2000 and the terminology used in ISO 9000:2000.

❏ Formal training on other requirements that are applicable to the organization. This would include government regulations for organizations producing regulated products such as drugs, medical devices, and aircraft. It also includes sector-specific requirements (for example, automotive, aerospace, telecommunications) and customer-imposed quality requirements.

❏ Training specifically targeted at the kind of internal auditing to be performed in the organization, including actual audit practice.

❏ Training on organization-specific requirements, including the scope and contents of the quality management system.

❏ Observing audits performed by others in the organization.

❏ Auditing under the supervision of a qualified auditor, either the audit boss or another individual who is authorized to make the decision that the candidate is capable of conducting internal audits.

Training to Consider to Ensure Maintenance of Auditor Competence

❏ Updates on standards

❏ Updates on changes to internal requirements

❏ Best practices from other organizations or from internal staff

❏ Highlights from the past year

❏ Case study exercises

❏ Effective report writing and interviewing

ITEM 9 CHECKLIST—AREAS TO CONSIDER WHEN REVIEWING DATA RESULTING FROM INTERNAL AUDITS

Auditing for Compliance

❑ When we consolidate all deviations from requirements into one database, are there any trends?

❑ Are there any functions or processes that consistently have numerous audit issues?

❑ Are there generic training shortcomings (for example, with temporary workers)?

Auditing to Uncover Improvement Opportunities

❑ Are there best practices that could be applied elsewhere in the organization?

❑ Are all auditors seeking out opportunities for improvement?

❑ Are there any common threads in the opportunities uncovered?

❑ Are there any trends in process performance evident?

Auditing Individual Processes (for example, a Production Work Cell)

❑ Is there evidence of consistent understanding of the link between functions, from business plans through achieving customer satisfaction?

❑ Are there any general issues with tools or infrastructure?

Auditing Across Functional Lines

❑ Are there any common problems at process interfaces?

❑ Are there any systemic breakdowns common to several departments, for example, documentation?

❑ Are there any common communications issues?

❑ Are there any common personnel issues?

❑ Is there any evidence of consistent failure to meet requirements?

ITEM 10 CHECKLIST—EXAMPLES OF REQUIREMENTS TO CONSIDER FOR REFERENCE WHEN PLANNING AN AUDIT

Internal Requirements

- ❑ Standard operating procedures
- ❑ Quality system procedures
- ❑ Training procedures
- ❑ Calibration procedures
- ❑ Start-up and shutdown procedures
- ❑ Maintenance procedures
- ❑ Emergency procedures
- ❑ Design procedures
- ❑ Records procedures
- ❑ Customer complaint procedures
- ❑ Specifications
- ❑ Drawings
- ❑ Advertising literature

External Requirements

- ❑ International trade agreements, such as the World Trade Organization
- ❑ International consensus standards, such as the ISO 9001:2000 document
- ❑ National regulations, such as the U.S. Code of Federal Regulations (CFR)
- ❑ National consensus standards, such as the ANSI Z1.11 standard for training and education
- ❑ Industry codes and standards, such as those promulgated by the American Association of Blood Banks or the Institute of Food Technology

❏   Package labels and inserts, found on regulated products and devices

❏   Corporate policy, designed to provide consistent direction across the enterprise

❏   Customer requirements, reflected in the contract and purchasing specifications

❏   Market and customer requirements for better products, improved services, or lower prices, that have been accepted by senior management as internal goals or requirements

ITEM 11 WORKSHEET—AUDIT PLAN DEVELOPMENT WORKSHEET

Audit Plan Template

Department	Start and stop date(s) and time(s) of the audit
Audit objectives	Audit scope

Audit Criteria

External requirements	Internal requirements
Auditor(s)	Audit interfaces and other resources required

Plan approval by:

ITEM 12 FORM—COLUMNAR FORM AUDIT CHECKLIST

Requirement	Yes	No	N/A	Notes
First question (reference)				
Second question (reference)				
Third question (reference)				
Fourth question (reference)				
and so on				

ITEM 13 FORM—FREE FORM AUDIT CHECKLIST

Audit checklist 23-03

1. First question is written here, across the entire page, using word wrap. At the end of the question, the reference is shown in parentheses. The question is followed by blank space to allow for handwritten notes in the field.

2. The second question follows the first in a similar fashion.

3. The third question follows.

4. And so on.

ITEM 14 CHECKLIST—ACTIVITIES TO BE PERFORMED PRIOR TO STARTING AN AUDIT

❑   Clearly define objectives and scope for the audit.

❑   Identify team and assignments.

❑   Complete specific audit plan for the upcoming audit.

❑   Gather flowcharts or maps of the processes, areas and activities about to be examined.

❑   Conduct a review and preliminary analysis of the formal (documented) requirements.

❑   Establish communication and agreement with the parties about to be audited.

❑   Create work papers to define information needs.

❑   Define an initial idea of the time and resources that will be necessary to perform the remainder of the audit.

ITEM 15 CHECKLIST—ACTIVITIES THAT SHOULD BE CONSIDERED FOR EACH AUDIT

❑ Holding an opening meeting with the manager of the area to be audited

❑ Observing processes

❑ Observing final product, if applicable

❑ Asking questions (as developed during audit planning)

❑ Gathering objective evidence of the extent to which requirements are being met or not met

❑ Keeping great notes

❑ Analyzing objective evidence

❑ Synthesizing all that is seen and heard and draw conclusions

❑ Holding a closing meeting with the manager of the audited area

ITEM 16 CHECKLIST—THINGS TO DO IN EVERY OPENING MEETING

❏   Introduce all parties.

❏   Review the audit objectives and scope.

❏   Determine the general flow and assignments for data gathering (who will be with whom and when).

❏   Make arrangements for a closing meeting.

❏   Review safety concerns.

❏   Review housekeeping and communications (escorts, briefings, and so on).

ITEM 17 CHECKLIST—EXAMPLES OF AREAS TO CONSIDER WHEN OBSERVING ANY PROCESS OR FUNCTION

❑ What are the objectives of the work center, area, process, activity, function, or product being observed?

❑ How do these relate to the overall objectives of the organization? To the quality policy? Are they consistent? Is there alignment?

❑ Does everyone involved know what the customer requirements are (both internal and external)?

❑ Is there an understanding of what is necessary to meet (or exceed) those customer requirements?

❑ Are individuals performing the work correctly? Do they know what to do and have the means to do it, including documentation, time, and tools?

❑ Are the requirements for successful completion of work clear?

❑ How do individuals know that they have performed the work to requirements? Are process or product metrics in place and being used?

❑ What is done with data that are collected related to the product or process? Who analyzes it? For what purpose? Is there evidence of use of the analyzed data?

❑ How is continual improvement addressed for the activity being observed?

❑ What happens when deviations from requirements are found? What are the processes for:

  ❑ Correction

  ❑ Control of nonconforming product

  ❑ Disposition of nonconforming product

  ❑ Analysis for possible corrective action

  ❑ Use of the data for preventive action, when applicable

❏ Is there evidence of any best practices or approaches that can be applied elsewhere in the organization?

❏ Do the inputs to the process being observed meet specified requirements?

❏ Are requirements defined for the processes being observed and understood by internal suppliers?

❏ How is internal supplier performance measured? Is there a feedback mechanism to those suppliers?

❏ How is customer feedback (external or internal) solicited and used for the processes being observed?

ITEM 18 FORM—AUDIT INTERVIEW FORM

Topic	Notes
Introduction State your purpose. Verify that distractions are OK. Try to put the person at ease.	
Job and Task What tasks are being performed?	
Training and Experience What training and experience are needed for the tasks?	
Internal Requirements What manuals, procedures, and instructions are used?	
External Requirements What codes or standards apply to the tasks?	
Available Help Where can help be obtained, when necessary?	
Technical Question Ask a technical question or two about the task.	
Demonstration Watch the task as it is performed.	
Off-Normal Events Explore how they handle off-normal events.	
Recurring Problems Ask about any recurring problems or difficulties.	
State Your Conclusions Bring up any good or bad points. No secrets.	
Close Thank them for participating.	

ITEM 19 CHECKLIST—MINIMUM THINGS TO INCLUDE IN CLOSING MEETINGS

❑ A brief summary of what was examined and why (scope and objectives)

❑ An overall opinion on the application of the quality management system within the areas just examined

❑ Any positive practices observed

❑ Any occurrences of failure to comply with requirements, and whether such occurrences were isolated or systemic

❑ As necessary, sharing with the auditee the objective evidence to substantiate any occurrences of failure to comply with requirements

❑ Any unusual events or practices or anything unexpected that was observed

❑ Resolution of any areas of disagreement over objective evidence or auditor conclusions

❑ Explaining the process for corrective action on any significant adverse findings

ITEM 20 FORM—INTERNAL AUDIT REPORT

Group or area audited:	Dates of audit:	Audit Number:
Enter the name here.	*Dates here.*	*Assigned by audit boss.*

Background:

> *What did you examine and why? Who did the looking?*

Conclusions:

> *Write a short (1–2 paragraph) summary of what you saw and experienced. Are the necessary controls in place, known, practiced, and doing the job? Is the part of the system you audited effectively implemented? Is it effective in meeting requirements and objectives?*

Problem areas:

> *Any adverse conclusions (findings) should be summarized here. No more than one short paragraph per finding.*

Positive practices:

> *Any noteworthy conclusions (positive practices) should be summarized here. No more than one short paragraph each.*

Prepared by:	Approved by:	Date prepared:
Audit team leader.	*Any required approval.*	*Date here.*

ITEM 21 FORM—FINDING SHEET

Area or Department:	Process:	Audit number:
Name the department or functional areas involved with the finding.	*Name of the process or processes involved with the finding.*	*As assigned by audit boss.*

Requirement reference:

State the requirement and where it comes from.

Auditee:

List key contacts involved with the finding.

Finding:

Give a paragraph description of the finding followed by statements supporting it. Include data.

Customer related? ❏ If so, explain consequences for the customer.	Organization related? ❏ If so, explain the consequences for the organization.
Explanation of the impact or potential impact on the customer.	*Explanation of the impact or potential impact on the organization.*

Signature of auditor:	Reviewed with:	Date prepared:
Signature of preparer.	*Name of auditee with whom finding was reviewed.*	*Date here.*

ITEM 22 FORM—POSITIVE PRACTICE RECORD

Positive Practice

Describe the positive practice:

> *Give a summary paragraph describing the positive practice. State how the practice provides superior results. List the observed facts and supporting data related to the positive practice.*

Information or other processes or activities supporting the positive practice:

> *Auditor and/or auditee statement of other processes or activities that are needed to operate the positive practice and achieve the results.*

Willingness to share the practice, processes, and results:

> *Statement of the extent to which the auditee is willing to share the results and support transfer of the positive practice to other parts of the organization.*

Auditor:	Auditee:
Signature of auditor.	*Signature of auditee.*

ITEM 23 FORM—BEST PRACTICE RECORD

Short name for this best practice:

Provide a brief subject line suitable for use in a best practices database.

Department or function:	Contact:	Date prepared:
Give the name of the department or functional unit of the organization responsible for the best practice.	*Name, address, phone, and e-mail address of the key contact for additional information.*	*Date here.*

Description of the results achieved:

Describe the actual results that were achieved by using the best practice. Provide numerical data and, if possible, comparisons of data before and after implementation of the best practice.

Description of the best practice:

Describe the practice in detail. Provide a summary statement and details of implementation. Provide process flowcharts, practice descriptions, and other information that an uninitiated reader will need to fully understand how you achieved the superior results.

Supporting processes:

Description of the supporting practices, activities, or processes that are essential for the best practice to effectively achieve the results.

ITEM 24 QUESTIONS—TYPICAL AUDIT ITEMS FOR COMPLIANCE WITH ISO 9001:2000

This is a list of questions taken from *ISO 9001:2000 Explained,* Second Edition, that can be used as reference during preparation of audit working papers. The list is not intended for use as an audit checklist but rather as a resource to be used in the development of checklists that are tailored to individual processes and circumstances.

Clause 4.1 Quality management system—General requirements

- Have the processes needed for quality management been identified?

- Have the sequence and interaction of these processes been determined?

- Have criteria and control methods been determined for control of the processes in the quality management system?

- Is information available to support the operation and monitoring of the processes?

- Are processes measured, monitored, and analyzed, with appropriate actions taken to achieve planned results and continual improvement?

- Is the quality management system established, documented, implemented, maintained, and continually improved?

- Has provision been made to ensure control of quality management system processes that are outsourced?

Clause 4.2.1 Documentation requirements—General

- Have documented procedures been prepared where specifically required by ISO 9001:2000?

- Is the extent of quality management system documentation dependent on the size and type of the organization?

- Is the extent of quality management system documentation dependent on the complexity and interaction of processes in the organization?

- Is the extent of quality management system documentation dependent on the competence of personnel in the organization?

Clause 4.2.2 Documentation requirements— Quality manual

- Does the organization have a quality manual that describes the interaction of the processes in the quality management system?

- Does the quality manual either include or reference the documented procedures describing the processes of the quality management system?

- Does the quality manual include the scope of the quality management system, including details of and justification for any exclusions taken under clause 1.2?

- Is the quality manual a controlled document?

Clause 4.2.3 Documentation requirements— Control of documents

- Has a documented procedure been established for document control?

- Are documents approved for adequacy prior to use?

- Are documents reviewed and updated as necessary?

- Are document changes reapproved to ensure adequacy prior to use?

- Is current document revision status maintained?

- Are relevant versions of applicable documents available at points of use?

- Is there a process to ensure that documents remain legible, readily identifiable, and retrievable?

- Are documents of external origin identified and their distribution controlled?

- Are obsolete documents retained for any purpose suitably identified to prevent unintended use?

Clause 4.2.4 Documentation requirements— Control of records

- Is there a documented procedure for the control of records?

- Have the organization's records been identified?

- Have retention times and disposition requirements been determined for all records?

- Are records disposed of as required by the organization's documented procedures?

- Have storage and retrieval requirements been determined and implemented for records?

- Have protection requirements been determined and implemented for records?

Clause 5.1 Management responsibility— Management commitment

- Has top management established a quality policy?

- Has top management developed quality objectives?

- Do top managers regularly perform management reviews and assess opportunities for improvement?

- Does top management provide and regularly review the adequacy of resources?

- Is there evidence of top management commitment to continually improve QMS effectiveness?

Clause 5.2 Management responsibility— Customer focus

- Is top management involved in the process of determining customer requirements and ensuring that they are met?

- Is there a process to ensure that employees understand the importance of meeting customer, regulatory, and statutory requirements?

Clause 5.3 Management responsibility—Quality policy

- Has a quality policy been developed?

- Does the quality policy include commitment to meeting requirements and commitment to continual improvement?

- Does the quality policy provide a framework for establishing and reviewing the quality objectives?

- Are quality objectives quantified?

- Has top management determined that the quality policy meets the needs of the organization and its customers?

- Is the policy communicated to and understood by all in the organization?

- Are the members of the organization clear as to their role in carrying out the policy?

- Is the quality policy included in the document control process?

- Is the quality policy reviewed for continuing suitability?

Clause 5.4.1 Management responsibility—Planning—Quality objectives

- Have quality objectives been established at each relevant function and level in the organization?

- Do quality objectives include those needed to meet requirements for the organization's products or services?

Clause 5.4.2 Management responsibility—Planning—Quality management system planning

- Has the organization identified the activities and processes required to meet objectives? Quality management system processes? Product or service realization processes? Verification processes? Exclusions under clause 1.2?

- Does quality planning include continual improvement of the processes of the quality management system?

- Does quality planning take into account the needs of the organization as changes occur?

Clause 5.5.1 Management responsibility— Responsibility, authority and communication— Responsibility and authority

- Are the organization's functions defined and communicated to facilitate effective quality management?

- Are responsibilities and authorities defined and communicated to facilitate effective quality management?

Clause 5.5.2 Management responsibility— Responsibility, authority and communication— Management representative

- Has top management appointed one or more management representatives within the quality management system as appropriate?

- Has top management defined the responsibilities and authority of the management representative?

- Does the management representative ensure that the processes of the quality management system are established and maintained? How?

- Does the management representative report to top management on the performance of the quality management system?

- Does the management representative promote awareness of customer requirements throughout the organization?

Clause 5.5.3 Management responsibility— Responsibility, authority and communication— Internal communication

- Do discussions with employees at all levels indicate that the organization effectively communicates about the processes of the quality management system and their effectiveness?

Clause 5.6.1 Management responsibility— Management Review—General

- Does top management review the quality management system at planned intervals to ensure its continuing suitability, adequacy, and effectiveness?

- Are management review records maintained?

Clause 5.6.2 Management responsibility— Management review—Review input

- Do the management reviews include evaluation of the need for changes to the organization's quality management system, including quality policy and quality objectives?

- Does management review input include: results of audits, customer feedback, process performance, product conformity, status of preventive and corrective actions, follow-up actions from earlier management reviews, changes that could affect the quality management system, and recommendations for improvement?

Clause 5.6.3 Management responsibility— Management review—Review output

- Do the outputs of management reviews include actions related to the improvement of the quality management system and its processes?

- Do the outputs of management reviews include actions related to the improvement of product related to customer requirements?

- Do the outputs of management reviews include resource needs?

Clause 6.1 Resource management— Provision of resources

- Has the organization determined the resources necessary to implement the quality management system?

- Has the organization provided the resources necessary to implement the quality management system?

- Has the organization determined the resources necessary to improve the effectiveness of the quality management system?

- Has the organization provided the resources necessary to improve the effectiveness of the quality management system?

- Has the organization determined the resources necessary to meet customer requirements?

- Has the organization determined the resources necessary to enhance customer satisfaction?

- Has the organization provided the resources necessary to enhance customer satisfaction?

Clause 6.2.1 Resource management— Human resources—General

- Are personnel who perform work affecting product quality competent based on education, training, skills, and experience?

Clause 6.2.2 Resource management—Human resources—Competence, awareness and training

- Does the organization identify the competency needs of the individual personnel performing activities affecting quality, including additional training needs?

- Does the organization provide training or take other actions to satisfy these needs?

- Does the organization evaluate the effectiveness of the training provided or of other actions taken to ensure competency?

- Does the organization ensure that employees are aware of the relevance and importance of their activities and how they contribute to the achievement of the quality objectives?

- Does the organization maintain records of education, experience, training, and qualifications?

Clause 6.3 Resource management—Infrastructure

- Does the organization identify, provide, and maintain the work space and associated facilities it needs to achieve conformity of product?

- Does the organization identify, provide, and maintain the equipment, hardware, and software it needs to achieve conformity of product?

- Does the organization identify, provide, and maintain the supporting services it needs to achieve conformity of product?

Clause 6.4 Resource management—Work environment

- Does the organization identify the conditions in the work environment that must be controlled to achieve conformity of product?

- Does the organization manage the human and physical factors of the work environment needed to achieve conformity of product?

Clause 7.1 Product realization—Planning of product realization

- Is there evidence of planning of production processes?

- Does the planning extend beyond production processes to encompass all product realization processes?

- Is the planning consistent with other elements of the quality management system?

- Does product realization documentation exist?

- Are product realization resources and facilities defined during the planning process, and do they appear to be adequate?

- Does the planning define the records that must be prepared to provide confidence in the conformity of the processes and resulting product?

Clause 7.2.1 Product realization—Customer related processes—Determination of requirements related to the product

- Does the organization determine customer requirements?

- Does the process include the determination of requirements needed but not specified?

- Are records available that provide evidence that customer requirements have been determined?

Clause 7.2.2 Product realization—Customer related processes—Review of requirements related to the product

- Does a process exist that requires the review of identified customer requirements before commitment to supply a product to the customer?

- Does a process exist that requires the review of quotes and orders to ensure that requirements are adequately defined?

- Is there a process for handling the review of verbal orders?

- Is there a process to handle the resolution of differences between quotes and orders?

- Does a process exist for handling changes to product requirements?

- Are records maintained of the results of reviews and actions taken?

Clause 7.2.3 Product realization—Customer related processes—Customer communication

- Are there effective processes in place to communicate with customers about product information, inquiries, contracts, order handling (including amendments), and customer feedback, including customer complaints?

Clause 7.3.1 Product realization—Design and development—Design and development planning

- Are the stages of the design and development project defined? Where?

- Are verification and validation addressed? Are these activities appropriate?

- Is it clear who is responsible for what?

- Are the communications channels and interfaces defined and managed? Is there evidence that communication on projects is occurring and that it is effective?

Clause 7.3.2 Product realization—Design and development—Design and development inputs

- Are requirements for new products defined and records maintained?

- Are the requirements complete?

- Are the requirements unambiguous?

- Are the requirements without conflict?

Clause 7.3.3 Product realization—Design and development—Design and development outputs

- Is the output of design and development projects in a form suitable for verification against inputs?

- Does the design and development output satisfy input requirements (for example, as stated in a functional requirements specification)?

- Does output provide, as appropriate, information for purchasing, production operations, and service provision?

- Are product acceptance criteria clearly stated?

- Are product safety and use characteristics identified?

- Is there an approval process for the release of products from the design and development process?

Clause 7.3.4 Product realization—Design and development—Design and development review

- Are design and development reviews being performed?

- Are they indicated in the project planning documents?

- Who attends?

- Is the attendance appropriate?

- Are results documented?

- Are follow-up actions taken?

- Are appropriate records maintained?

Clause 7.3.5 Product realization—Design and development—Design and development verification

- Is a verification process in place?

- Is it effectively implemented?

- Are follow-up actions recorded?

- Are required records defined and maintained?

Clause 7.3.6 Product realization—Design and development—Design and development validation

- Is design and development validation performed to confirm that the product is capable of meeting the requirements for intended use?

- Is validation completed prior to delivery, when applicable?

- Are suitable controls provided in cases where full validation cannot be performed prior to delivery?

- Are records of design and development validation maintained?

Clause 7.3.7 Product realization—Design and development—Control of design and development changes

- Are all design and development project changes documented and reviewed?

- Are design and development changes verified and validated, as appropriate?

- Is there evidence to demonstrate that changes are authorized?

- Do records include the results of reviews of changes?

- Have changes been communicated to interested parties?

- Do records include follow-up actions related to the review of changes?

Clause 7.4.1 Purchasing—Purchasing process

- Have criteria for the selection and periodic evaluation of suppliers been defined?

- Is there a process for selecting and evaluating suppliers?

- Are the results of evaluations documented and retained as records?

Clause 7.4.2 Purchasing—Purchasing information

- Do purchasing documents adequately describe the products being ordered?

- Do purchasing documents include, where appropriate, requirements for approval or qualification of product, procedures, processes, equipment, and personnel?

- Do purchasing documents include, where applicable, quality management system requirements?

- How does the organization assure the adequacy of specified purchase requirements prior to communication to the supplier?

Clause 7.4.3 Purchasing—Verification of purchased product

- Has the organization defined a process for verifying that purchased product conforms to defined requirements?

- Is the process effectively implemented?

- Does objective evidence exist of product acceptance?

- Is verification of purchased product performed at the supplier's premises? If so, are the arrangements specified and does objective evidence exist of effective implementation?

Clause 7.5.1 Production and service provision— Control of production and service provision

- Are specifications available that define quality characteristic requirements of the product or service?

- Has the organization determined the criteria of acceptability for demonstrating the suitability of equipment used for production and service operations to meet product or service specifications?

- Has the organization demonstrated the suitability of equipment used for production and service operations to meet product or service specifications?

- Has the organization defined all production and service provision activities that require control, including those that need ongoing monitoring, work instructions, or special controls?

- Are work instructions available and adequate to permit control of the appropriate operations so as to ensure conformity of the product or service?

- Have the requirements for the work environment needed to ensure conformity of the product or service been defined, and are these work environment requirements being met?

- Is suitable monitoring and measurement equipment available when and where necessary to ensure conformity of the product or service?

- Have monitoring and measurement activities been planned and are they carried out as required?

- For hardware, processed material, and software: have suitable processes been implemented for release of the product and for its delivery to the customer?

- Have suitable release mechanisms been put in place to ensure that product or service conforms to requirements?

Clause 7.5.2 Production and service provision— Validation of processes for production and service provision

- Has the organization determined which production or service processes require validation? Have these processes been validated?

- Has the organization defined criteria for the review and approval of production or service processes? Have the reviews and approvals been performed?

- Has the organization determined what personnel need to be qualified and has it determined the qualification criteria? Have these personnel been qualified?

- Does the organization use defined methods and procedures to validate processes?

- Have the requirements for records of validated processes been defined?

- Are records of validated processes maintained?

- Have the processes requiring revalidation been defined?

- Have processes, as required, been revalidated?

- Do adequate records exist to assure that process validation is effectively implemented?

Clause 7.5.3 Production and service provision—Identification and traceability

- Has the product been identified by suitable means throughout production and service operations?

- Has the status of the product been identified at suitable stages with respect to monitoring and measurement requirements?

- Is traceability a requirement?

- Where traceability is a requirement, is the unique identification of the product recorded and controlled?

Clause 7.5.4 Production and service provision—Customer property

- Has the organization identified, verified, protected, and maintained customer property that is provided for incorporation into the product?

- Does control extend to all customer property, including intellectual property?

- Does the organization have records that indicate when customer property has been lost, damaged, or otherwise found to be unsuitable?

- Is there evidence that when customer property has been lost, damaged, or otherwise found to be unsuitable, the customer has been informed? Are records maintained?

Clause 7.5.5 Production and service provision—Preservation of product

- Does the organization uniquely identify product during internal processing and delivery?

- Does the organization handle the product during internal processing and delivery so as to preserve conformity to customer requirements?

- Does the organization package the product during internal processing and delivery so as to preserve conformity to requirements?

- Does the organization store the product during internal processing and delivery so as to preserve conformity to requirements?

- Does the organization protect the product during internal processing and delivery so as to preserve conformity to requirements?

Clause 7.5.6 Production and service provision—Control of monitoring and measuring devices

- Has the organization identified the measurements to be made?

- Has the organization identified the monitoring and measurement devices required to assure conformity of product to specified requirements?

- Are monitoring and measurement devices used to ensure measurement capability?

- Are monitoring and measurement devices calibrated and adjusted periodically or before use against devices traceable to international or national standards?

- Is the basis used for calibration recorded when traceability to international or national standards cannot be done, since no standards exist?

- Are monitoring and measurement devices safeguarded from adjustments that would invalidate the calibration?

- Are monitoring and measurement devices protected from damage and deterioration during handling, maintenance, and storage?

- Do monitoring and measurement devices have the results of their calibration recorded?

- Does the organization reassess validity of previous results from monitoring and measurement devices if the devices are found to be out of calibration? Is corrective action taken?

- Is the software used for monitoring and measurement of specified requirements confirmed as to its suitability before use?

Clause 8.1 Measurement, analysis and improvement—General

- Is objective evidence available to demonstrate that the organization has defined, planned, and implemented the monitoring and measurement activities needed to assure conformity and to achieve improvement?

- Is objective evidence available to demonstrate that the organization has determined the need for and use of applicable methodologies, including statistical techniques?

Clause 8.2.1 Measurement, analysis and improvement—Monitoring and measurement—Customer satisfaction

- Is customer satisfaction information monitored?

- Are methods for gathering and using customer information determined and deployed throughout the organization?

Clause 8.2.2 Measurement, analysis and improvement—Monitoring and measurement—Internal audit

- Does the organization conduct periodic audits of the quality management system?

- Do the periodic audits evaluate the conformity of the quality management system to the requirements of ISO 9001:2000?

- Do the periodic audits evaluate the degree to which the quality management system has been effectively implemented and maintained?

- Does the organization plan the audit program taking into consideration the status and importance of areas to be audited?

- Does the organization plan the audit program taking into consideration the results of previous audits?

- Are the audit scope, frequency, and methodologies defined?

- Do the audit process and auditor assignment ensure objectivity and impartiality?

- Is there a documented procedure that includes the responsibilities and requirements for conducting audits?

- Is there a documented procedure that describes how to ensure the independence of auditors?

- Is there a documented procedure for reporting results and maintaining records?

- Is timely corrective action taken on deficiencies found during the audit?

- Do follow-up actions include the verification of the implementation of corrective action?

- Do follow-up actions include the reporting of verification results?

Clause 8.2.3 Measurement, analysis and improvement—Monitoring and measurement—Monitoring and measurement of processes

- Have the key quality management system processes, especially the product realization processes, needed to meet planned results been identified?

- Are suitable methods used to measure and monitor these key processes?

- Are the intended purposes of the key processes quantified by process parameter specifications, by specifications for the product output of the process, or by some other means?

- Are the monitoring and measurement methods for processes of the quality management system adequate for confirming the continuing suitability of each process to satisfy its intended purpose and achieve its planned result?

Clause 8.2.4 Measurement, analysis and improvement—Monitoring and measurement—Monitoring and measurement of product

- Does the organization measure and monitor product characteristics to verify that product requirements have been met?

- Does the organization measure and monitor product characteristics at appropriate stages of the product realization process?

- Is there objective evidence that acceptance criteria for product have been met?

- Do records identify the person authorizing release of the product?

- Are all specified activities performed before product release and service delivery?

- If there are instances in which all specified activities have not been performed before product release or service delivery, has a relevant authority, or as appropriate the customer, been informed and approved of the action?

Clause 8.3 Measurement, analysis and improvement— Control of nonconforming product

- Is there a documented procedure to assure that product that does not conform to requirements is identified and controlled to prevent unintended use or delivery?

- Is there evidence of appropriate action being taken when nonconforming product has been detected after delivery or use has started?

- Is it required that any proposed rectification of nonconforming product be reported for concession to the customer, the end user, or a regulatory body?

- Is there objective evidence of appropriate communication with a customer when the organization proposes rectification of nonconforming product?

- Are concessions obtained from customers as appropriate?

Clause 8.4 Measurement, analysis and improvement— Analysis of data

- Has the organization determined the appropriate data to be collected?

- Does the organization analyze the appropriate data to determine the suitability and effectiveness of the quality management system?

- Does the organization analyze appropriate data to identify improvements that can be made?

- Does the organization analyze appropriate data to provide information on customer satisfaction?

- Does the organization analyze appropriate data to provide information on conformance to product requirements?

- Does the organization analyze appropriate data to provide information on characteristics of processes, products, and their trends?

- Does the organization analyze appropriate data to provide information on suppliers?

Clause 8.5.1 Measurement, analysis and improvement— Improvement—Continual improvement

- Does the organization plan and manage processes necessary for the continual improvement of the quality management system?

- Does the organization use quality policy, quality objectives, and data analysis to facilitate the continual improvement of the quality management system?

- Does the organization use audit results, corrective action, and preventive action to facilitate the continual improvement of the quality management system?

Clause 8.5.2 Measurement, analysis and improvement—Improvement—Corrective action

- Does the organization take corrective action to eliminate the causes of nonconformities?

- Is the corrective action taken appropriate to the impact of the problems encountered?

- Do documented procedures for corrective action provide for identifying nonconformities, determining causes, evaluating the need for actions to prevent recurrence, determining the corrective action needed, and the implementation of the needed corrective action?

- Do documented procedures for corrective action provide for recording the results of corrective actions taken?

- Do the documented procedures for corrective action provide for reviewing the corrective action taken?

Clause 8.5.3 Measurement, analysis and improvement—Improvement—Preventive action

- Does the organization identify preventive actions needed to eliminate the potential causes of possible nonconformities?

- Is preventive action taken appropriate to the impact of potential problems?

- Do the documented procedures for preventive action provide for identifying potential nonconformities and their probable causes?

- Do the documented procedures for preventive action provide for determining the need for preventive action and the implementation of the preventive action needed?

- Do the documented procedures for preventive action provide for recording the results of the preventive actions taken?

- Do the documented procedures for preventive action provide for reviewing the preventive action taken?

Further Reading List

ANSI/ISO/ASQ Q9000-2000, *Quality management systems—Fundamentals and vocabulary*. Milwaukee: American Society for Quality, 2000.

ANSI/ISO/ASQ Q9001-2000, *Quality management systems—Requirements*. Milwaukee: American Society for Quality, 2000.

ANSI/ISO/ASQ Q9004-2000, *Quality management systems—Guidelines for performance improvement*. Milwaukee: American Society for Quality, 2000.

Arter, Dennis R. *Quality Audits for Improved Performance*. Milwaukee: ASQ Quality Press, 2002.

ASQ Quality Audit Division, J. P. Russell, editing director. *The Quality Audit Handbook*, Second Edition. Milwaukee: ASQ Quality Press, 2000.

BSR/ISO/ASQ QE19011-2002, Proposed U.S. adoption of International Standard ISO 19011:2002, Guidelines for quality and/or environmental management systems auditing. Milwaukee: American Society for Quality, 2002.

Cianfrani, Charles A., and John E. (Jack) West. *Cracking the Case of ISO 9001:2000 for Manufacturing*. Milwaukee: ASQ Quality Press, 2002.

———. *Cracking the Case of ISO 9001:2000 for Service*. Milwaukee: ASQ Quality Press, 2002.

Cianfrani, Charles A., Joseph J. Tsiakals, and John E. (Jack) West. *The ASQ ISO 9000:2000 Handbook*. Milwaukee: ASQ Quality Press, 2002.

———. *ISO 9001:2000 Explained*, Second Edition. Milwaukee: ASQ Quality Press, 2001.

West, John E. (Jack), and Charles A. Cianfrani. *ISO 9001:2000 An Audio Workshop and Master Slide Presentation*, Second Edition. Milwaukee: ASQ Quality Press, 2001.

ISO/TC 176 PRODUCT INTRODUCTION AND SUPPORT PACKAGES FOR ISO 9001:2000

ISO/TC 176, the international committee responsible for the ISO 9000 family of standards has published and periodically updates a set of Introduction and Support documents for ISO 9001:2000. These may be obtained, free of charge from the following Web site: www.bsi.org.uk/iso-tc176-sc2 .

The following lists Introduction and Support documents available as of December 2002:

ISO/TC 176/SC 2/N525R, ISO 9000 Introduction and Support Package: Guidance on the Documentation Requirements of ISO 9001:2000.

ISO/TC 176/SC 2/N524R3, ISO 9000 Introduction and Support Package: Guidance on ISO 9001:2000 clause 1.2 *"Application."*

ISO/TC 176/SC 2/N544R, ISO 9000 Introduction and Support Package: Guidance on the Process Approach to quality management systems.

ISO/TC 176/SC 2/N526R, ISO 9000 Introduction and Support Package: Guidance on the Terminology used in ISO 9001:2000 and ISO 9004:2000.

Index

A

analysis of control systems, 116
analyzing information, 106
audit alternatives, 37–38
audit analysis, 123–24
audit basis, 89
audit boss,
    assigning, 51
    audit follow-up, 139–40
    and best practices, 137–38
    defining purpose statement, 80
    proactive role, 143
    responsibilities, 56–58, 63–65,
        69–73
audit characteristics, 42–43
    meeting ISO 9001:2000
        requirements, 42
    for performance improvement, 43
audit checklists, 94–95, 164–65
audit, closing, 129–30
audit closure, 78, 129–40
    audit boss's responsibility for
        follow-up, 139–40
    audit issues to action requests,
        130–31
    closing the audit, 129–30
    correcting nonconformities, 133
    corrective action process, 133–34
    developing corrective action
        requests, 132–33

    developing preventive action
        requests, 134–35
    documenting best practices,
        137–39
    preventive action process, 135–36
audit concepts, 3–5
audit criteria, 85–89, 152–53, 161–62
    external requirements, 86–87,
        161–62
    internal requirements, 87–88, 161
audit, cross-functional, 38
audit data and analysis, 69–73, 160
audit data, reevaluating, 142
audit, defined, 3, 5
audit emphasis, 82
audit follow-up, 139–40
audit interview, 104–5, 171
audit issues to action requests, 130–39
audit objectives, 41–45, 79–80, 99,
    152–53
audit performance, 77, 97–114, 167
    analyzing and reaching
        conclusions, 106–7
    asking questions, 104–5
    auditor characteristics, 108–10
    caution areas, 111–13
    closing meeting, 107
    gathering objective evidence, 105
    no documented procedures, 103
    observing processes and results,
        101–3

C

caution areas,
    things auditees do to auditors,
        112–13
    things auditors do to auditees,
        111–13
chartering, internal audit program,
    49–51
closed questions, 105, 109
closing meeting, 107, 172
closing the audit, 129–30
columnar form of audit
    checklist, 94
communicating, internal auditing,
    51–52
compliance audits, 41, 70, 79
conclusions, reaching, 106–7
confidentiality, 8–9
conflict, 110
conformity assessment audits, 41–42
consequences, 119–20
continual improvement, 119
controls, process, 30
correcting nonconformities, 133–34
corrective action process, 133–34
corrective action requests, 131,
    132–33, 134–35
cross-functional audit, 38
customer audits of suppliers, 42
customer feedback, 31
customers, 30, 79–80

D

data, analyzing and sorting, 118, 122
data, assembling, 117–18, 121–22
data, recording, 105
data, reevaluating audit, 142
documentation, 32–36, 92–93
documentation approach to quality
    management systems, 32
documented procedures, 34–36
    lack of, 103–4
documenting best practices, 137–39
documenting examples of excellence,
    137–39
documents, 90–93
duty to report, 9

E

ethical principles, 8–9, 66–67
evidence-based focus, 7
excellence, documenting examples of,
    137–39
exit meeting, 124–25

F

factory processes, 91
facts, 117–18
feedback, 31
finding sheets, 116, 174
finding statement, 120–21
findings, 116–17
flowcharting, 91–92
follow-up on audit results, 11
free-form layout of audit checklist,
    94–95

H

horizontal audit, 37, 81, 149–51

I

inputs and suppliers, 30
integrated audit programs, 50
internal audit personnel, 59–60
internal audit procedures, 53,
    54–55, 155
internal audit process, establishing,
    52–53
internal audit program, chartering,
    49–51
internal auditing, communication,
    51–52
internal quality audits, 3, 49–50
    reasons for, 49–50
ISO 19011:2002, 5, 6, 51, 54, 126
ISO 9000:2000 clauses,
    4.1, Quality management
        system general
        requirements, 19–20,
        21–22
    5.4, Planning, 19, 20